DR. KENNETH R. LENZ, MBA CPA PHD

Transforming Entrepreneurs

Christian Entrepreneurs Who Transformed Our World

First published by Entrepreneur Leadership Institute 2021

Published in Pleasant Garden, North Carolina by Entrepreneur Leadership Institute. Library of Congress Control Number 2021913100

Library of Congress Cataloging-in-Publication Data is available upon request.

For more information and to purchase books and courses, visit us at www.EntrepreneurLeadership.net

First edition

ISBN: 978-1-7359810-3-1

*This book was professionally typeset on Reedsy.
Find out more at reedsy.com*

Contents

Praise for "Transforming Entrepreneurship"

"Finally an insightful real world example of how Christian entrepreneurs are doing God's work! Informative, captivating, and truly motivational."

—Mark Salman, CEO
Skidril Industries LLC

"About time someone started chronicling the "Acts of the Entrepreneurs!" Ken thoughtfully and briskly takes you through a journey that falls through the cracks of business and church history. What were the unseen motivations and drives that led these men and women to abundant service and success? It certainly was not a "separation of business from faith." Calculated risk takers should be seen as vital members of the body of Christ, not just the business world. If ever there were men and women living out being Jesus' hands and feet, where would we be without those whose self-sacrifice and creativity brings society much opportunity? And the opportunities Christian Entrepreneurs create transcend the millions of temporal and financial benefits; for they bring mercy, charity, and mass planting of Gospel seeds for the Church to help water. If you are thirsty to create a product or service profitable and become a stronger hand or foot for

Jesus, then don't put this book down."

—Rev. Kermit Rickenberg
Executive Director of Support for Missions, Inc
A non-profit dedicated to aiding missions with
entrepreneurship.

I

This Changes Everything

The rise of entrepreneurship

1

This Changes Everything: Transforming Entrepreneurship

"Do not be conformed to this world, but be transformed by the renewal of your mind, that by testing you may discern what is the will of God, what is good and acceptable and perfect."
Romans 12:2

This Changes Everything

In a world full of poverty, racism, gender inequality, and tragedy, we are all in desperate need of the hope and goodness that God alone can provide. When Jesus sacrificed Himself on the cross, he changed everything. He offers total transformation to each and every one of us. And when we let Him transform our hearts and lives, he equips us—by the truth of His Word and the power of His Holy Spirit in us—to transform the world around us.

For Christians, entrepreneurship isn't just about making money or experiencing success. For those who have been transformed by God, entrepreneurship is an opportunity to transform the lives of employees, customers, communities, and societies across the globe. Transformation is seamlessly woven into the Christian's entire way of life.

This book focuses on this special niche of entrepreneurs who both improve society and share the Gospel message in word and deed alongside mere job creation—pointing to their assurance of eternal reward, as well as temporal enhancements to quality of life.

Coca-Cola, Mary Kay, and the YMCA.

What do these businesses have in common? Two core things: These businesses transformed the world as we know it, and they were built by Christian entrepreneurs.

They're not the only ones.

Heinz, The Associated Press, and monasteries and nunneries around the world—Yes, they're businesses too!—were formed by Christian entrepreneurs.

Your business could be added to the list of companies like these. Your name could be among the Christian entrepreneurs who transform society.

Many things we take for granted today are the hard work of enterprising individuals who dreamed big, applied creative yet highly practical ideas, risked their own finances, and refused to yield any ground to adversity. The modern world we live in is, in no small part, the legacy of people like you who took great risks, persevered, and did the right thing. Follow in their footsteps, and you are on the path to leaving a legacy of your own.

How to Use This Book

This is a book of mentors. Study these pages. Imitate the qualities and habits that made them successful. Avoid their mistakes. Learn from how they responded to their challenges and rebounded from their errors. But also recognize that they were human beings, using God-given talents to the best of their ability. Their strengths, weaknesses, failures, and successes all form a great testament to how a Christian can live out a Christian life as he conducts business.

Some of the entrepreneurs in these pages were lovable individuals, while others were criticized for their harsh personalities. Regardless, they all have two things in common: 1) They all possess entrepreneurial leadership qualities. 2) They are all Christians who take God's Word seriously. Both characteristics are essential to developing major, creative, Godly improvements in society.

There is no artificial barrier between Sunday and Monday for these Christian entrepreneurs: No separation between church and business. The Christian's religious concerns are not separated from their business interests. Rather, they are intricately intertwined. And the one informs the other, as Paul

5

the Apostle notes in Romans 12:2:

> Do not be conformed to this world, but be transformed
> by the renewal of your mind, that by testing you may
> discern what is the will of God, what is good and
> acceptable and perfect.

The entrepreneurs in this book did just that. They let God transform their minds in a way that, in turn, transformed their lives and businesses: Monday through Sunday, 24/7.

This is what can happen when people whose minds have been transformed by the Gospel become entrepreneurs: Business becomes more than just something to make money. For the Christian who believes in and lives out the Biblical principle of "Commit your work to the Lord, and your plans will be established."[1] business becomes something that transforms lives, communities, societies, and the world.

And we too have the opportunity to partner with God in this kind of transformation when we first let Him transform our lives, hearts, and minds.

How is Christian Entrepreneurship Transforming?

For those of us who come from the perspective of living in the United States of America, it has been observed that there is a synthesis between Christianity and American business, and

---

[1]   The Holy Bible, English Standard Version, Proverbs 16:3

particularly American entrepreneurial success. As a visitor to America, Alexis De Tocqueville, observed in the 1800s that "the spirit of liberty" and "the spirit of religion" combine in a unique way in the United States. The same holds true today.

Every small business provides jobs. In some ways, American's ongoing entrepreneurial culture is part of the process of creating "little platoons" of society in a business context that Alexis De Tocqueville wrote about long ago. Many add various types of innovation. They all contribute to both the tax base and spreading prosperity in their communities through the transactions they engage in. The Christian understanding of "helping one's neighbor" through employment and bettering the world he lives in for his fellow man is perhaps most alive and well within an entrepreneurial culture informed by Christian ethical principles.

According to the Small Business Administration (SBA), in 2016, the United States had nearly thirty million small businesses (defined as up to 500 employees). Over 50 percent of the entire working population—more than 120 million people—work for small business owners.

For nearly all of the past 400 years of American history, throughout boom times and bust, an enormous number of small businesses commence operations each month—currently more than 543 thousand monthly or over 2.9 million yearly. While the failure rate is high, at least half survive five years, a third for ten years, and a quarter thrive for fifteen years or more.

Some key statistics stand out:

- These business owners create 70 percent of all new American jobs—even when large corporations reduce their workforce or outsource to overseas companies.
- They generate more than half of the non-farm gross domestic product.[2]
- SBA's Office of Advocacy research also found that smaller companies are much more likely to develop emerging technologies than larger companies.
- They also produced sixteen times more patents per employee than large patent-generating corporations.
- Smaller companies account for approximately 8 percent of patents granted.
- Twenty-four percent of those patents come in the top one hundred emerging clusters of new technology.

All of this is just a glimpse into the profound influence of company founders. It indicates the enormous impact entrepreneurial companies have on new technology and emerging industries far beyond their mere initial size.

Statistics And Impact

What do all these statistics indicate about the impact of entrepreneurs? Entrepreneurial firms' impact is greater than

---

[2] Despite the 36 percent higher governmental regulatory burden on smaller firms versus large companies.

just job creation. Entrepreneurial firms are crucial to the health and growth of the American economy. They are vital to the continued affluence of Americans and the foreigners these entrepreneurial companies conduct business with.

Studies conducted by the Philanthropy Roundtable clearly indicate Christians provide the majority of both cash donations and volunteer time to both religious and secular charities. A recent study found that charitable contributions of time and money correlated closely to the frequency of church service attendance.

Ernst & Young, a top global accounting firm, conducted a survey in 2010 for Fidelity Charitable Gift Fund, finding entrepreneurs allocate twice the percentage of profits to charity than America's largest companies, with 26 percent incorporating corporate philanthropy into their original business plans.

- Nearly 70 percent supported charities before achieving wealth.
- Seventy-three percent of entrepreneurial companies surveyed actively encourage employees to volunteer their time and expertise, while 53 percent subsidize or supplement financial charitable donations.
- Sixty-one percent currently sit on charitable boards, and 50 percent either are serving or have served in the past as chairperson or top officer of a charity (including the many charities started by these entrepreneurs).
- A vast majority of entrepreneurs rate the business benefits of charitable activities as very low or no priority for them:

In other words, they are interested in charitable work for the sake of helping others, not for any publicity or marketing benefits that might be gained.

- Most preferred to give in a "low key" manner, with 53 percent citing three motivations: gratitude for the help received, empathy for those less fortunate, and achieving the financial freedom to afford generous gifts of time and money.

This charitable impact does not include the additional social entrepreneurship efforts that Christian entrepreneurs engage in to improve social, environmental, and spiritual conditions. Entrepreneurs tend to concentrate charitable efforts in the local communities where they live and conduct business, although some venture globally.

Quiet social entrepreneurial efforts might range from hiring unskilled welfare recipients and patiently working with them to develop healthy job and household management skills (as a group of Raleigh, North Carolina business owners has been doing for many years) to anonymously help with medical and other significant bills for employee families and community neighbors, and to provide Biblical information to customers, vendors, employees, and others.

The impact of Christian entrepreneurs has a ripple effect throughout their local communities and often far beyond. The impact of some of the Christian entrepreneurs you will meet in these pages extends across the globe and across centuries.

Their efforts changed the fabric of society.

How? Because not only did these entrepreneurs and their businesses have a direct impact on the world, they had an indirect impact. So many indirect impacts are hard to measure—like the way a business through its ethics can transform the hearts and minds of men and women and the life-changing choices they make. Others are easier to see.

By producing goods and services that are taxed, they build the government tax base. By hiring and retaining more employees than are essential, they create more jobs. By engaging in charitable efforts, they reduce the need for government expenditures and meet needs in their communities. By connecting with vendors, they create economic activity, which boosts yet more job creation, taxable activity, and possibly more generous charitable donations from the owners of their vendor companies. Through indirect impacts like these, they generate a further rise in the prosperity of their communities.

We can do the same.

Before we meet the entrepreneurs that transformed the world as we know it, we need to understand the world as it was before. We need to understand the men and women before them that set all of this in motion. I'd like you to meet the pre-entrepreneurs:

I'd like to introduce you to the saints and pirates.

2

Part One: Saints, Accounting, and the Rule of 72

"I alone cannot change the world,
but I can cast a stone across the water
to create many ripples."
Mother Theresa

Introduction

What do you think of when you think of an entrepreneur? A small business? Historically, Babylonia, Assyria, China, Egypt, India, Persia, and Greece all had artisans and traders who built very small businesses and occasionally achieved great wealth but not high social status. That was because ancient societies made distinctions between farming—which was considered a highly respected occupation in nearly all older societies—versus the trader or merchant group.

Roman and Greek Societies

Rome may have been the first society to organize formal commercial districts. These districts encouraged greater small business activity, the societal structure of laws, road networks, merchant fleets, and other infrastructure. All of this supported and formally encouraged greater commercial activity.

The Phoenicians, however, were the exception in early world history. Their vast Mediterranean empire required writing, accounting, and management skills, which sometimes brought status as high as nobility.

In keeping with the Greek and Roman philosophers' teachings, smaller commerce was considered a less desirable and sometimes disdainful occupation. Back then agriculture was considered the key to stable wealth and large amounts of leisure time that marked a more honorable and successful lifestyle. On the other hand, there were tradesmen, who were considered better than slaves and freedmen (liberti) but were far below the patrician class in both political and social status. However, a few tradesmen became wealthy.

Two key factors inhibited greater innovation in the ancient world: consistent legal code and slavery. If merchants and tradesmen could not fully count upon the rule of law, they had less incentive to develop technological innovation that propels civilization forward. In fact, the vast majority of Roman subjects and subjects in other empires lived at bare subsistence level and the largest societal group was slaves. Slavery and the abuse of politically emasculated people, held

13

back commercial progress because it discouraged innovation, business development and even surplus food production.

Chinese court documents highlight the political elite's negative attitude towards merchants, underscoring the global extent of this harmful attitude. Considering this pervasive attitude, it is unsurprising that historical records indicate no increase in the gross domestic product (GDP) for any society before 1000 AD. Even after 1000 AD, the rise in GDP for most nations did not exceed one-half of one percent annually until 1820, and then only for some countries, according to Bernstein's research reported in his book *The Birth of Plenty*.

Over time, merchants and freedmen were given a form of second-class citizenship—never full participatory rights in political power. In this climate, the fact that the Apostle Paul became an early model of an entrepreneur is an indication of the respect the merchant class would hold within the history of Christianity. The Apostle Paul established both individual congregations and much of the entire church infrastructure throughout the Mediterranean—an early form of social entrepreneurship. He accomplished this while supporting himself with his famous tent-making business, thus developing the first self-sustaining marketplace ministry model. Other Biblical figures have started businesses, but Paul provides the first role model for large-scale sustainable development.

There were still a few examples of emerging entrepreneurial activity during this multi-millennial era of pre-entrepreneurship. Paul was such a precursor. Founders of the second monastic order and the first order of nuns could be considered similar entrepreneurially-inclined individuals who rose above the discouragement against such efforts. Entrepreneurship and Christianity were governed closely by the Christian understanding of ethical business practices.

We will meet three such individuals who not only followed in his footsteps but went a step further. They built on this ground a foundation for the Christian entrepreneurs who would come after them—a foundation for the entrepreneurs we will meet in the coming pages of this book and a foundation for you. The first of these three is Luca Bartolemeo de Pacioli.

Luca Bartolomeo de Pacioli

A Franciscan monk and math tutor for Leonardo da Vinci, Luca Bartolomeo de Pacioli[3] is credited as the father of accounting. He wrote the "Summa de Arithmetica, Geometria, Proportioni et Proportionalita" in 1494. In this book, he described the double-entry bookkeeping system and developed the initial concepts of the balance sheet and income statement, which are still foundational elements of modern accounting. Friar[4] Pacioli is said to have been born in Sansepolcro, Tuscany, into a merchant family. He published his famous accounting and mathematics treatise while living in Venice, the commercial powerhouse of the 15th century, before moving to Milan.

---

3 Circa 1447-1517.

4 A member of any of certain religious orders of men, especially the four mendicant orders: Augustinians, Carmelites, Dominicans, and Franciscans.

Pacioli discovered the Rule of 72, which is a calculation of compounded interest used to estimate expected investment returns which are then compared against possible losses to give business owners a reasonably accurate understanding of whether a proposed transaction is a potentially worthwhile risk or not. He even discussed the topic of accounting ethics: He insisted that closing entries and a trial balance be used each day. This was to assure accurate and timely information. It also helped to identify any potential theft or deceit quickly.

His system of double-entry bookkeeping opened the door to tracking larger operations and enterprises.

It is the basis of all financial record-keeping today.

As we will see later in this chapter, Saint Teresa will use Pacioli's system to track the financial progress of all her nunneries.

St. Pachomius

Pachomius[5] was born a peasant, conscripted into the imperial Roman army, and fought in at least one series of battles conducted in northern Egypt. During his tour of army duty, he encountered Christians for the first time in and near the war zone. He was attracted to how the Christians he encountered were so kind—regardless of their circumstances and irrespective of the ill-treatment they received from soldiers.

---

[5] Circa 290 to 350 AD.

As a result, Pachomius converted to Christianity and became an enthusiastic advocate of Christianity among both Christians and pagans alike. His ideas were referred to as Cenobitism. He and his followers were called the Desert Fathers, primarily because they chose to leave the civilized towns to live in isolated, desolate, parched areas.

Before long, he received an angelic vision inspiring him to develop a more intensely introspective approach to his ministry and a calling to build a place for similar-minded men. He and his followers constructed the very first monastery on Tabenna[6], where he received his angelic vision.

It was a small building with a wall to keep out curious visitors. Unlike the first monastic order whose followers simply lived in caves or out in the open desert with little to no communication between themselves, Pachomius insisted all monks learn to read to participate in standardized worship services twice per day. The cenobitic lifestyle was strict and primitive, focusing on growing closer to Jesus and renouncing the world's concerns.

To avoid these concerns, Pachomius and his followers developed a commercial enterprise. They sold mats, shoes, and other personal goods and tools at below-market prices to help people—most of whom lived in poverty at that time.

Saint Pachomius had quirks that some might question while

---

[6] A desert island in the middle of the upper Nile River in Egypt, south of Alexandria.

others admire. For example, he would not admit any Christian priest into the monastic order because he wanted it to remain a layman's movement, open to the common man. His contemporaries recorded that he was most noted for his long, frequent praying and his great love for his fellow monks. The saintly monastic enterprise he founded lasted for several centuries, growing into thousands of monks building several large monasteries.

This self-sufficient Christian study and charity model is still with us today. For example, Belgian monasteries are prized for their world-class beer production, which has enabled them to engage in spiritual development while maintaining their independence from state-run church bodies and societal, economic, and spiritual challenges.

Saint Teresa

The realm of Entrepreneurship was in no way closed to women. Christianity welcomed innovation by allowing women, particularly women working within the monastic system, relative autonomy to implement enterprising business structures. Christianity's greater emphasis than its contemporary religions on rule of law as giving glory to God, and the negative effects of slavery on a society, helped enable this acceptance of women in business, particularly the business of God.

A key example is that of Saint Teresa, born in 1515 in Avila, Spain. Early in her life, Teresa joined a lax convent for daughters of wealthy men. One day, Teresa wrote about discovering the "laws of spiritual gravity," a vision occurring during a chapel prayer time. From then on, she experienced many visions throughout her life. From them, she learned and expressed a desire to do the divine will, not be rapt in ecstasy and cloistered away from worldly problems like the escape provided by all known convents of her era up to that point.

Teresa established the first order of nuns and built her first convent in Toledo, Spain. She called this new organization the Carmel order[7], or Carmelites, honoring the ideas of the earlier order of monks. Until that time, priests ran the convents, and the young ladies living there had not necessarily dedicated their lives irrevocably in service to God.

The nuns joining Teresa's order modeled their approach of a self-sustaining religious non-profit organization to consciously follow as spiritual descendants of those first hermits on Mount Carmel. They depended upon the sale of their handiwork to support themselves, but the price was left to the discretion of the purchaser—just like Pachomius's commercial enterprise.

Unlike Pachomius, who trained monks to start similar yet independent monasteries elsewhere, Teresa built an order of nuns with a chain of convents throughout Spain and neighboring nations. They were small: No convent community was allowed to have more than 13 members. So, as soon as she established one convent house, she moved on and founded another. In a

---

[7] Bertold of Calabria founded the original order of Carmel in Palestine in 1155.

way, this was an early franchising model.

According to her followers, Teresa excelled at detailed and strong management skills. She attended to every nuance of daily activities in each convent and sought to standardize daily routines for all nuns in all locations.

She had a servant leader approach: She led by example, including all menial tasks. She was flexible with any opposition to her ideas—even disagreements within her new order.

Teresa used Pacioli's double-entry method for accurately tracking transactions and reporting results, allowing her to build and run efficient operations at a lower risk than had been possible before then. She also insisted that visitors could inspect every part of the convent, including the financial records—a radically new idea of transparency, not only for the Middle Ages but for recorded human history. Like a company has accountability to shareholders, these monastic communities had accountability to other Christians.

Her first challenge in building her new organization was to overcome the mediocrity and apathy so prevalent in the culture of her time. Her response was to create "interior castles" of inner personal strength within each nun and inspire followers to intercede in prayer for the people of the world without becoming infected by the apathy and the humanism (i.e. man-centered moral drift) of her century.

Eventually, Teresa's new order expanded into France and other nations. Then, a division was started for men. Now, the

Carmelite order included both monks and nuns in separate facilities but often working together to renew the original Carmel order to become witnesses for Jesus to all of society. One sister described convent life as a citadel of prayer for others. The concern was to save other people's souls, not through outward evangelism efforts but through prayer and penance.

3

Part Two: Wars, Shipmasters, and Pirates

"A ship in harbor is safe —
but that is not what ships are built for."
John A. Shedd

Changing Tides

Trading over any significant distance has almost always been dangerous and expensive. Throughout world history, enterprising individuals had to balance risk and reward. This calculus was particularly dangerous in the ancient world. While there were stable empires such as China, Babylon, Persia, and others, merchants were not protected from robbers when traveling. The big exception was the Roman Republic and later the Empire, that had a vested interest in protecting trade, including along what would become known as the Silk Road.

However, after Rome's collapse[8], trading was largely restricted to local transactions. The Crusades[9] opened a large demand and opportunity for greater trading over a much wider territory, protected to some extent by Christian knights. And merchants were gradually expanding their network of trading partners, spurred partly by the desire for new or exotic goods brought to their attention by returning crusader knights. Another factor was war.

Entrepreneurial-minded shipmasters might have developed as early as the 14th century. However, the Bubonic Plague or Black Death[10] shut down most trade and set back the emergence of entrepreneurs by several centuries. The Hundred Years War[11] between the English House of Plantagenet and the House of Valois for control over France plus the War of the Roses[12] between dueling branches of the Plantagenet family over kingly control of all England and Wales wreaked havoc on the populous concurrent with the Bubonic Plague.

Agriculture was devastated, causing vast hunger and such a drop in tax revenue that it threatened both the landowners and the ability of kings and noblemen to sustain their developing governments. These wars also had another effect: Such large-scale wars required not just aristocratic fighters. They needed

---

[8] 476 AD

[9] 1095-1291

[10] 1346-1353, killing an estimated 75 to 200 million Europeans, or 30 percent to 60 percent of the continent's entire population.

[11] 1337-1453

[12] 1455-1487

vast commoner armies not seen since Roman times. This led to eroding feudalism and a growing feeling of pervasive nationalism.

Profiteers, Shipmasters, and Pirates

Changing societal conditions opened new opportunities. As noted earlier, merchants were gradually expanding their network of trading partners. Shipmasters used that new nationalism mindset and the need for alternative food and tax revenue to negotiate profitable trades between factions while avoiding or defeating the increasing number of pirates and privateers arising from the mounting disorder. Since kings could rarely raise enough revenue to support a navy, they typically outsourced naval battles to private shipmasters.

Kings offered this highly profitable opportunity by issuing a document called Letters of Mark and Reprisal. These were common from the 12th to the early 19th centuries: Shipmasters agreed to attack ships belonging to or supporting the king's enemies in exchange for a double portion of the profits earned by selling the captured vessels and goods.

For some shipmasters, the lure of war profiteering was so great that they turned pirate, attacking any ship—regardless of national loyalties. Geoffrey Chaucer[13], the famous English poet, included in one of his plays the story of a shipman from Dartmouth who was not only a pirate but also rose to the rank

---

[13] Circa 1343 to 1400.

of gentry and nobility. This reflects the leadership abilities of these shipmasters to achieve wealth, status, royal favor, and occasionally gained authority over noblemen.

Shipmaster status was one of the very few occupations in the Middle Ages that provided the potential to rise in social status and wealth. The typical path was to sign on as a lowly sailor, advancing in a shipboard position by proving sailing and negotiation skills. Eventually, some earned the rank of ship's captain, which involved both recruiting and managing the crew and overseeing sailing courses and negotiating both sales of cargo and purchase of supplies in very diverse ports.

Suppose a captain proved himself highly valuable to investors. In that case, he might negotiate a contract for portage rights, which allowed the captain or shipmaster to transport his own cargo at no cost, along with sharing in a set percentage of profits.

If the shipmaster was wise in his transactions, he could eventually save enough to buy a partial ownership interest in his ship. The most entrepreneurial ones built profitable net-works of contacts both domestically and abroad. This enabled them to purchase an entire ship of their own. Eventually, a few developed a fleet of ships with perhaps ownership in a shipbuilding enterprise.

The Shipping and Merchant Trading is Finally Set

The 16th century was when the outlines of true entrepreneurship first began to become discernible, particularly in England. From the 14th century onwards the merchants of Venice gradually developed large merchant fleets to nearly duplicate the ancient trading empires of the Romans and the Phoneticians.

Groups of merchants in Northern Europe gradually created the Hanseatic League, headquartered in Lubeck, now part of Germany. This merchant trading and shipping network was a confederation of independent city-states, but the League had its navy to defend members' cargo ships. Eventually, the League extended its trading network to as far away as England and most of the northern European seaports and occasional more distant ports of call.

By the 16th century, English shipmasters had developed considerable shipping opportunities of their own. The English government's respect for individual freedom[14] had gradually grown. The serfdom system slowly receded to the point where many individuals were able to build and sail commercial shipping vessels to make more profitable use of their connections with Hanseatic League members, French merchants, and Venetian trading ships.

Through many disputes with sailors, vendors, partners, merchant customers, government officials, and other shipmasters,

---

[14] King John signed the Magna Carta Libertatum, the "Great Charter of the Liberties" in 1215.

the English shipmasters gradually developed the legal principles of Admiralty law. You might consider admiralty law as
the naval equivalent of the Common law commercial code.

Conclusion

To be clear, rapid wealth accumulation and climb in social
status would be rare until the early 19th century. There were
undoubtedly individuals with the characteristics and inclina-
tions of Christian entrepreneurs leading up to this. However,
few records remain describing these pre-entrepreneur pio-
neers. Even fewer sources provide their names, let alone any
Biblically-minded efforts by any of them to help others.

Yet, just as in the final days of winter when we see little or no
signs of spring coming, all the elements for change and growth
are happening below the surface. Several critical factors
emerged during this era that were—and still are—required
for entrepreneurs to flourish.

The 16th century in England was also the time of a series of religious disruptions, beginning with King Henry VIII[15], followed
by fluctuating between Catholic and Protestant sway over the
country. Tyndale[16] translated the first English Bible, which
provided God's Word to the masses of ordinary people. This
spurred renewed devotion to living out an authentic Biblical
lifestyle modeled after Jesus; not to mention an outpouring of

---

[15] 1491-1547

[16] 1494-1536

entrepreneurial activity surrounding the invention and use of the printing press in modern society!

By the 17th century, a growing number of people, particularly in England, were freed from serfdom. Simultaneously, a renewal of Christian faith was once again reaching ever deeper into the ranks of ordinary people. In response, the development of ideas and enterprises sprung into action.

John Bunyan[17] wrote Pilgrim's Progress as an allegory of a righteous life during this same century, which integrated secular concerns and challenges with spiritual issues—a viewpoint the church had moved away from during the late Middle Ages.

The tides were changing. The vital elements that remained to develop a societal environment where entrepreneurship could finally boom were about to arrive.

---

[17] 1628–1688

4

Missing Pieces, Vital Ethics, and The Rule of Law

*"Freedom prospers when religion is vibrant
and the rule of law under God is acknowledged."*
Ronald Reagan.

Missing Pieces

Missing pieces remained. Pieces necessary for entrepreneurship to finally thrive. They would not come together until around the early 19th century.

These missing elements had a strong ethical or morality-based foundation. They eventually came to be collectively referred to as a *"laissez-faire* market system," or simply "capitalism."

Throughout the next three chapters, we will review the Biblical basis for this free market system, which lets entrepreneurship flourish, and the specific factors proven over time to support entrepreneurial innovation. Not every factor ties back directly to a biblical principle. Still, the nature of entrepreneurial endeavors is a more ethical, caring approach than the self-ish socialist system, which tends to inhibit entrepreneurial improvements, become unsustainable, and ultimately lead to societal collapse. Socialism fundamentally presumes that there can be no increase of either supply or a fundamental alteration of the demands of human existence (including things such as longer life-spans). As such, it stifles the entrepreneurial spirit and punishes those who would seek change, even change for the collective good.

Vital Ethics

What are the key ingredients to success? And what are the rules of the game? As we have discussed in previous chapters, the rule of law and the emancipation of society from systems of serfdom and slavery were key drivers of historical and societal change. What do they have in common?

Ethics. Specifically Christian Ethics. While the concept of a Christian ethical framework may in itself be offensive to some, a Christian ethical framework is, without parallel, the surest ethical footing for a future entrepreneur.

Innovating and taking risks in entrepreneurship requires vital ethics. What ethical factors are required? The book *Why Nations Fail* provides two broad outlines, the inclusive and the extractive models. The inclusive model requires separation of political and business leadership groups and fluid movement within each group (leadership frequently changes with families moving in and out of these controlling groups).

An extractive model ossifies leadership by permitting a few families to maintain leadership control in both the political and business groups, leading inevitably to lawless theft and oppression of a powerless majority, who quickly lose all motivation for productivity or even for maintaining infrastructure.

The key to this study is whether leadership is spread throughout society to assure enough balance for a stable rule of law environment versus a predatory approach of extracting the work of others until there is nothing left or the abusive leadership is violently overthrown.

Nations can move into and out of one model towards the other, so neither failure nor success is assured over the long term. Extractive political institutions are fragile with internal fighting over a fixed or declining economic productivity. They can temporarily grow, but that growth is not sustainable due to inherent lawlessness.

In his book Birth of Plenty, Bernstein gives a more specific list. He notes four societal factors required to encourage the entrepreneurial spark that generates increasing widespread prosperity.

The first is reason. Reason involves the willingness to question established assumptions logically. This requires true critical thinking skills to improve efficiency and effectiveness in solving a problem.

The second is capital. Capital involves assets like money, equipment, or land needed to fund or expand a startup company. Many business academics decry the capital shortage. However, while some savings are certainly necessary for the entrepreneur to pay their own monthly bills to fuel high growth, most of the entrepreneurs profiled in this book built their enterprises starting with very little capital.

The third is speed. Speed involves both the rate of transport for goods as well as communication. When the government inhibits the free transfer of ideas and products, the cost of those products increases and less innovation occurs. The internet and a general worldwide gradual movement towards greater freedom over the past half-century have made it far easier for capital, ideas, and goods to flow to where demand is greatest.

The fourth factor is property rights. Private individual property rights enforcement—more commonly called the Rule of Law—is a particular challenge mentioned prominently in both books. It is also the only factor primarily dependent upon the government.

It is essential to understand this most critical environmental factor necessary for entrepreneurs to create societal enhancements.

Rule of Law

Rule of law is defined carefully by Fredrick Bastiat[18] in his book *The Law* as natural law versus political law. Bastiat defines natural law by explaining that each of us has rights granted directly by God to defend our person, liberty, and property. All are aware of the values impressed upon them. The role of the state is to provide a common or massed force to assist individuals in defending each person's rights as God intends.

Some examples would be expressing an opinion in public, enforcing voluntarily entered contractual rights, a parliament (or legislature) setting a tax rate, sending an army to defend citizens against invasion, or approving budgeted expenditures supporting the common defense of natural rights.

Bastiat did not originate the concept of natural law or rule of law. Rather, he was part of a vibrant and ongoing tradition of natural law thinkers. America's Founding Fathers expressed similar conceptions of natural law in both the Declaration of Independence and the Constitution. Before that, English Common Law had gradually developed a body of legal precedents, which had begun being codified starting sometime around the 13th century. English Common Law itself found its basis in older natural law thinkers, particularly that of Greece and Rome.

During those centuries of development, Common Law certainly added some concepts that were not consistent with

---

[18] 1801–1850

biblical ideals. However, Bastiat restated and summarized these ideas, explicitly pointing out that while political law is fickle and ever-changing (according to the opinions of people in power at any given moment), natural law[19] is a fixed and immovable set of reference points provided by Jehovah which cannot be modified or voided by mere mortals, not even a human legislature, since these rights and responsibilities are both granted directly by God to each individual and impressed upon each person's soul.

With the certainty that God provides the natural law or rule of law principles, entrepreneurs have the confidence to engage in risky commerce, knowing what the consequences will be for each type of action and providing the ability to estimate probable results. Entrepreneurs also have the surety of understanding probable results of transactions across human political boundaries since the God of the Bible is King over all humanity. Outside the general principles of natural law, however, as the old saying goes, results may vary.

Entrepreneurship requires a biblically-provided environment to commence and grow to a substantial degree. The principles of fair play—that rules will be applied fairly and uniformly—is fundamental to basic risk calculations and risk-taking. A society that structures its legal system in a Biblically literate way allows those within that society to bring societal and eternal benefits to other people as Jesus called them to do.

And when people don't play by the rules of the game? Well,

---

[19] Or law of nature and nature's God.

when humans, acting either as individuals or in a governmental capacity, violate these rules, entrepreneurs can seek court redress or avoid transacting business. A key ingredient to success—Christian ethics—enables entrepreneurs to better society: where they observe injustice or violations of God's call to treat one another with fairness and care as illustrated in the Bible they have a socially accepted means of recourse.

5

"The Devil" vs. The Father of Economics

"If [justice] is removed, the great,
the immense fabric of human society,...
must in a moment crumble into atoms."
Adam Smith

Champions

An opponent of the *laissez-faire* market system coined the term "capitalism" only a few decades after entrepreneurship began to flourish. The older authoritarian ideology of socialism, based upon a very different set of moral assumptions, presented their worldview in a fresh new framework.

In practice, socialism is a form of impractical Christian heresy, which among other effects, prevents entrepreneurship and the moral and temporal blessings entrepreneurial endeavors generate. Both worldviews are worth studying to discern clearly what moral basis and environmental variables will encourage entrepreneurship and its resulting greater prosperity for most people.

We will explore the two concepts through their champions—"The Devil" and "The Father of Economics."

The Devil

To his friends and family, he was known as "Moor" for his Moorish complexion of bronzed skin and dark eyes. To others, he was known as simply "Charley." To those close to him, he was known, fondly, as "The Devil."

You probably know him as Karl Marx: proponent of Marxist theory and champion of Socialism.

There are many significant flaws in Marx's socialist theory that can impact entrepreneurs. It's important that we understand these potential challenges and how they can affect the businesses we create.

We'll start with what the free market enterprise system—mistakenly called capitalism—is not. Marxist theory defines "capitalism" as a system of private commodity exchanges. It is private ownership and control over the means of production, where the surplus product becomes a source of unearned income for its owners. The owner of the means of production are called both capitalists and bourgeoisie. In Marx's theory, the capitalists and bourgeoisie derive their "surplus product" by appropriating value from their workers. In harsher terms,

37

by stealing.

In contrast, socialism is the means of production owned by the society as a whole, with the surplus product being a source of income for the whole society. Fundamentally, this raises the virtue of equality, both of action (generation of value) and outcome (ownership) to the chief virtue of the State. That may seem to be an oversimplification, and there are nuances within Marxist theory and economics ever since.

According to Marx and his colleague Friedrich Engels,[20] the definition of "value" is sometimes the "use-value," (which they acknowledge is indeterminable) and sometimes the "exchange-value" (determined by its "socially necessary labor" time). In other words, when a business owner who holds title to the equipment, facilities, money, and other resources required to conduct business risks those assets to make a potential—but not guaranteed—profit, Marx values only the workers' labor.

Thus in any exchange-value between commodities,[21] the "value" should be calculated as the difference in the time it took to harvest or build one commodity versus another. Anything beyond that calculation is supposed to represent "profit" that Marx defines as theft by the business owner of the workers' labor.

---

[20] 1820-1895

[21] Marx does not seem to recognize services can be a separate salable "commodity."

The fallacy in this worldview is the unproven assumption that the business owner does not risk any assets—in other words, capital—that he or she has worked hard for and saved for overtime, nor any recognition of the owner's own labor and creative use of the mind God provided to the business owner.

Socialist theory devalues the owner's contributions to zero, thus claiming any profit comes from exploiting others by owning the "means of production" as superior to the "means of labor."

Briefly, there are several other significant flaws in Marx's socialist theory that impact entrepreneurs. Effective resource allocation—let alone maximally efficient resource allocation—cannot be determined because socialist "accounting" methods have no objective way to decide what goods should be produced. Or where to send scarce resources. With no key indicators like supply and demand—how is a market to know what to produce? State planners will have to step in to determine the needs, lack of needs, and presumed lack of needs, of any given population at any given time.

This form of "accounting" totally ignores consumer or populous demand for certain products or services above others. Unlike Pacioli's double-entry bookkeeping invention, which provides accurate measurement combined with ethical accountability, planners are not held responsible to even the simplest standardized account principles. Worse, this system does not respond to the pressure of changing conditions in the same way as a free-market enterprise system. "Account" wrongly for an unexpected drought, resulting in no harvest, and well, there is no bread. You can easily fill in the rest of this line of reasoning.

We mentioned earlier that Socialist theory represents a Christian heresy. How? It claims that "Each contributes according to his abilities and takes only according to his needs." In reality, human nature leads individuals to care for only those assets they own, not other people's property or property owned by the state (i.e., nobody). The tragedy of the commons, an example that used to be presented in many economics classes, demonstrates this principle most clearly.

Socialist systems found that workers tend to do the minimal amount of work they are forced to while taking all the "free" stuff they can get since there is no cost applied directly to each individual (although there is a great cost to "society" or spread among everyone). Worse, there is no possible method to determine risk and reward under this system, so nothing can be efficiently produced. Only a central planner whose guesses are implemented by force or government threat of violence against the workers they supposedly are trying to help has any impact upon the system.

Marx took this concept of common "communion" or sharing from Acts 2:44:

"And all who believed were together and had all things in common."

Still, the vast difference between socialism and Christian charity is the early church Christians shared from their privately owned assets voluntarily in response to recognizing God's love for them—not from watching the product of their hard work get stolen to be forcibly redistributed by a distant politician. And the greed that socialism produces in a population certainly is against the spirit of the Christian understanding of communion.

Socialism inevitably has consumed all the accumulated wealth of any society where rulers implemented it, so coercive force quickly becomes required to obtain enough work to slow down the consumption of all resources and delay the inevitable gradual collapse. Both the impractical unworkability of this system and its inherent systemic selfishness-promoting immorality thwart entrepreneurial improvements for everyone, leaving every person much poorer and enslaved.

Marx did not invent the envy-driven idea of socialism. In *New Deal in Old Rome,* Henry Haskell documents how socialism was tried on an epic scale during the late Roman republic. In fact, it was tried in every single one of the dictatorial empire stages of that civilization. How did it go?

Socialism led to the fall of Rome.

The Father of Economics

Now, we will explore the concept of the free-market enterprise system through the eyes of Adam Smith. This will help us understand both the concept of this system and the way it can be considered an extension of Biblical ethics.

Smith lived and developed his free-market ideas at the dawn of the industrial revolution. Born in June 1723, Adam Smith's father died just before his birth. He would be raised by his mother, who wanted him to become a priest. At age 14, he entered the University of Glasgow in his native Scotland but did not graduate, leaving at 17. He then attended Oxford University's Balliol College, graduating in 1746, and returned to Scotland to become a popular lecturer in English literature at the University of Glasgow.

Smith lived and developed his free markets ideas, at the dawn of the industrial revolution.

In 1750 Smith was appointed lecturer of logic, as well as signing his agreement with the Westminster Confession of Faith, reflecting his strong interest in metaphysical questions which eventually lead him to pursue the chair of Ethics in 1751, staying in that position for the next thirteen years before becoming Dean of Faculty in 1760 followed by Vice-Rector in 1762.

During the years he taught ethics, England suffered from a declining intellectual climate and morals. This decline was later challenged and partly reversed by William Wilberforce,[22] the great Christian morals reformer and champion for outlawing slavery throughout the British Empire, himself the son of a wealthy merchant.

Other major influences on English morals came from the

---

[22] 1759-1833

successful American Revolution[23] versus the failed French Revolution.[24] Smith taught Natural Theology for the first half of his ethics chair tenure, which included proofs of the being and attributes of God and principles of the human mind upon which religion is founded.

Contemporaries questioned whether Smith was truly an orthodox Christian because his lectures reflected too much of the Aristotle-oriented thoughts of fellow Scottish philosopher and economist scholar David Hume[25] in his moral inquiries. However, Smith clearly believed in the Biblical message. Later on, you will understand how he saw the free-market enterprise as an extension of Biblical ethics.

Smith's first book entitled *Theory of Moral Sentiments*[26] and his other famous book—*An Inquiry into the Nature and Causes of the Wealth of Nations*[27] both explained the moral, Biblically-oriented essence of the economic system we now refer to as capitalism. The first book explored the division between old and new English moralists. In brief, the older philosophers'[28] perceived rules were derived from self-interest. The more modern theorists[29] observed rules developing from intuition, recognized in good/right versus evil/wrong constructs like

---

[23] 1775-1783

[24] 1789-1799

[25] 1711-1776

[26] 1759

[27] 1776

[28] Hobbes, Mandeville, and Hume.

[29] Clarke and Price.

Euclid's axioms or by intellect (championed by the third Earl of Shaftesbury and Hutcheson), which the newer philosophers referred to as conscience.

Smith's syncretic or dialectic answer to both of these schools of philosophy was to claim morals are derived from both prudence and benevolence equally to create the virtuous character. Such virtue is required to achieve happiness (thus merging the Greek and Biblical ideas). Happiness is tranquility and enjoyment, which has no part of indolence or apathy, nor avarice and ambition.

This first book resulted from thinking about and engaging in scholarly discussions during his years of lecturing on ethics. In particular, his lectures on justice and police became the basis for his more famous second book. Both books underwent many revisions and reprintings throughout the remainder of his life.

Smith touted the "enlightened self-interest" concept of free enterprise. When people cooperate to make something, everyone is better off than if each tried to supply every need for his or her family.

The Invisible Hand, Corn Laws, and 2,000 pins

Smith coined the example of manufacturing a pin. If one man completed every step to make all the parts required (assuming each part would be available, which under the old feudal system many components could not be acquired in most of the country at any price), it would still take a full year and cost six pounds sterling to make a single pin.

By dividing the work into eighteen steps with a different worker in a plant completing each step, they could collectively make 2,000 pins per day at a dramatically lower sale price of sixpence—a 99.8 percent reduction in the cost! The profit for the factory owner could be substantial with only a modest profit margin by selling large quantities.

While the owner could pay higher wages than the worker could earn under the old feudal system, even if he was paid no more, Smith observed the worker's standard of living was still far higher because his wages now allowed his family to purchase many more goods of higher quality than the old feudal subsistence level approach permitted previously.

As the worker's skills increase, the owner gladly paid the more valuable worker higher wages to retain his higher productivity because both benefit from the higher output and higher quality. Hence, the price per unit continued to drop further.

However, there is resistance to this concept. Economists today recognize a concept called "rent-seeking." This idea, a common characteristic of socialist societies, results from a private party such as royalty, noblemen, or politically connected big corporate executives convincing politicians to pass laws protecting them from competition or granting them monopoly or another unfair advantage over competitors.

Smith noted that the cost of transactions above the "natural in Jersey City Colgate, he kept much of the business volume because of his bartered rate" (freely negotiated price)—in other words, the rent-seeking special privileges benefit—actually reduced public wealth and purchasing power for everyone.

During the 18th century, the British government enforced a system called mercantilism, which provided rent-seeking advantages to selected people at a substantial cost to the majority of others, particularly colonialists.

Smith vigorously refuted mercantilism, insisting that one should determine wealth by the abundance of resources (efficiency), including—but not limited to—the commodity of money itself. This very egalitarian theory benefited the common person the most, not those able to gain wealth through government-enforced help.

Smith likewise opposed taxes that were intrusive and expensive to collect, such as income, customs, excise, and similar taxes. He favored taxes that were easily determined, such as land taxes. After his lifetime, Smith's ideas were proven dramatically.

The Corn Laws[30] imposed high import duties on food and grains (called corn), guaranteeing high profits for large landowners at the expense of the commoners. Urban residents resented the high food prices, which peaked during the Irish famine of 1845-1852. Some form of import tariff on food had

---

[30] 1815-1846

46

been in place since 1689, but the corn laws took landowner greed to an extreme.

Throughout this period, English subjects were widely known for their lawlessness, and customs officials were known for their corruption. Shortly after the repeal of this onerous law, food became plentiful, and prices dropped substantially. Since there were no longer any import duties or restrictions, there was no need to bribe customs officials, nor necessity to raid royal forests to obtain food. This led to Englishmen gaining a high reputation for being law-abiding citizens in a few short years. In turn, this stabilized the rule of law, fostering an environment that encourages entrepreneurship.

God created us in His image. So, He built into each human a desire for justice. But by rejecting the true God, socialism insists on the impractical equality of results, ignoring that we are all endowed with differing skills, physical abilities, birth situations, mental capacities, and have differing willingness to adhere to God's commands.

Socialism leads to envy and forced redistribution away from productive people towards politically favored groups. Free enterprise emphasizes equal opportunity, recognizing that all will be better off while prospering at different amounts. While Adam Smith's ideas were only a beginning for developing a formal theory of free enterprise, they still form the basis of the free-market approach today.

The Socialist believes in things. The Capitalist believes in people. And people are capable of the soaring intangibles of ideas and spirit.

6

Creative Destruction, Philosophers, and the Constitution

*"Nothing is more powerful
than an idea whose time has come."*
Victor Hugo

Philosophers

Throughout this chapter, we will meet many men whose ideas built on Adam Smith's definition of capitalism and shaped the landscape of entrepreneurship. We will see how these ideas shaped a nation and transformed it into what it has become today.

There are some key players that you should know to get the full picture of the ongoing history of the definition of capitalism and the landscape of entrepreneurship. Together, let's cover a brief history of who they are and why they are important.

Joseph Schumpeter: 1883-1950

Joseph Schumpeter popularized the term "creative destruc-
tion" to describe the impact innovators make on industries
and the economy. He proposed that capitalism and prosperity
are inherent to Protestant religious values derived from the
Bible. He was the first economist to theorize this way about
entrepreneurship, building partly upon Max Weber's[31] development of sociology which was explained in Weber's book *The
Protestant Ethic and the Spirit of Capitalism.*[32]

Walter Lippman: 1889-1974

Walter Lippman said, "capitalism is based on an ideal that for
the first time in human history gave men a way of producing
wealth in which the good fortune of others multiplied their
own." He and other researchers noted that business people
are heroes because they generously give hope that continuing
scarcities and conflicts can be peacefully overcome. Lippman
stated, "... the materialist fallacy: the belief that wealth
consists chiefly not of human knowledge and creativity, generosity and love, but of a limited fund of 'natural resources,'
always in danger of running out..."

---

[31] 1864-1920

[32] 1905

Friedrich Hayek: 1899-1992 & Ludwig Mises: 1881-1973

Friedrich Hayek and Ludwig von Mises developed the Austrian school of economics. It differs from classical economic theory[33] in explaining price movements in the short term, but otherwise has much in common with Smith's viewpoint. Say's Law of Markets (a major classical economics theory) states production is the source of demand.

Austrian economics claims prices are a function of a voluntary agreement between buyer and seller unrelated to production costs. Each of these economists, basing their theories on applied real-world observations examined from within a Biblical-based worldview, recognized the behavioral aspects of the free enterprise system but did not quite identify the spark for societal improvement, which is not capital but innovative ideas.

Milton Friedman: 1912-2006

Milton Friedman and Thomas Sowell[34] were both part of the Chicago School, a group of free-market economists based in the University of Chicago. Friedman explained the intellectual refutation against the socialist Keynesian economic theory

---

[33] Which is the Smith-based Labor Theory of Value.

[34] 1930-current

championed by John Maynard Keynes[35].

Interestingly, Sowell was initially a Marxist who recognized the damage socialism caused and the prosperity free markets provided, which caused him to become a staunch advocate for the free-market enterprise. Both economists referred to the biblical basis of free-market concepts.

Harbey Leibenstin: 1922-1994

Harbey Leibenstin from Harvard describes his theory called X-efficiency, meaning the critical difference between socialist and capitalist productivity is motivation and spirit. Input does not determine output. He notes:

> Capitalism is based on the idea that we live in a world of unfathomable complexity, ignorance, and peril and that we cannot possibly prevail over our difficulties without constant efforts of initiative, sympathy, discovery, and love.

He notes that collective regulations deaden the moral spirit of risk-taking, leading entrepreneurs to face danger and fight for a better world.

---

[35] 1883-1946

George Gilder: 1939-current

George Gilder provides succinct clarifications into the Biblically-informed view of entrepreneurship, as both described and contrasted. For example, in his article *The Moral Sources of Capitalism* Gilder makes the following observations:

- "Capitalism is good and successful not because it miraculously transmutes personal avarice and ambition into collective prosperity, but because it calls forth, propagates, and relies upon the best and most generous of human qualities."
- "Capitalism begins with giving."
- "A gift will only elicit a greater response if it is based on an understanding of the needs of others."
- Say's Law Market requires giving first to get later. Accounts receivable requires faith in others.
- Socialism presumes to calculate the needs of others in an attempt to eliminate uncertainty, thus ruling out acts of faith so essential to innovation and progress, and upon which entrepreneurs build societal improvements.

Perhaps all of these research insights can best be summarized by paraphrasing the words of Jesus from Matthew 7:7: Give and you will be given unto; seek and you shall find; cast your bread upon the waters, and it will return to you many fold.

As you serve others in a free market system, hope and generosity lead to success.

The Constitution and American Entrepreneurship

Meltzer raises intriguing questions. He and other researchers note that in the freest societies (which are overwhelmingly free-market economies), the people in the top 1 percent change rapidly. Within any decade, while the overall income or wealth differentials may increase, the individual people included within that top wealth level have an average turnover of over 40 percent. In stark contrast, the wealth gap is just as wide in socialist economies, but the turnover of individual families at the top is almost non-existent. When it occurs, it is usually due to a violent action rather than a peaceful, gradual transition.

Considering these factors, it is not a coincidence that most entrepreneurs have come from the United States. Our Declaration of Independence and Constitution attempt to protect individual liberty and private property rights by limiting government officials' ability to impose an extractive or socialist type of economy, supporting great freedom of opportunity for each individual.

America's Founding Fathers performed an extensive amount of research on various governmental structures and moral principles throughout all recorded history to arrive at the set of principles and structure that has become the oldest constitution in the world due to the stability and freedom it affirms. According to the writings of many delegates to the Constitutional Convention, the Bible provided a framework for the ethical principles embedded in the Founding documents. Former Soviet chess grandmaster Garry Kasparov said:

Are we loyal to the principles of individual freedom, of faith, of excellence, of compassion, of the value of human life? These moral values are also the values of innovation and the free market, by the way. It is no coincidence that these founding American values created the greatest democracy in the world and also the greatest economy in the world.

He continued by comparing these American values to Jesus' Sermon on the Mount description of a shining city on a hill and a light unto the world, not a stagnant materialistic status quo. Likewise, the early church leader James emphasized the natural need to display inner faith through outward works as proof of a changed spirit.

It is not the material action of helping to meet the needs of others that makes the entrepreneur more spiritual or righteous, but instead, it is the reverse. A Godly viewpoint motivates the Christian entrepreneur to risk time, assets, and reputation for meeting other people's needs more efficiently and effectively.

As these men built on the ideas of Adam Smith and the Bible, we too can build upon their ideas to form businesses that transform both society and human hearts.

II

The Entrepreneurs

7

Diversifying Income Streams, Tithing, and Soap

"Honor Him by sharing what you earn.
Begin by tithing all you receive."
— A canal boat captain, to William Colgate

William Colgate

1783-1857

The first several chapters provided an overview of the impact, historical buildup, and ethical basis for the entrepreneurial age. Let us now explore specific examples of how individual Christian entrepreneurs used their God-given freedom and inspiration to successfully transform society for good and righteous improvements. A great place to start is with a true renaissance man involved in utilizing his wealth and time in a great number of charitable directions, even as his business diversified into other lines of consumer goods.

William Colgate descended from a strongly pro-liberty family. His father, Robert, was a yeoman in Kent County, United Kingdom. Kent had been a source of resistance against government tyranny from the time it was conquered by General Gaius Julius Caesar[36] through the Norman invasion in the 11th century, playing a major role in revolts such as the Peasants' Revolt of 1381, Jack Cade's rebellion of 1450, and Wyatt's Rebellion of 1554. The county seat of Canterbury has remained the capital of English Christianity since Augustine of Canterbury was sent in 597 to convert the pagans (starting with King Ethelberht) and oversee the building of Canterbury Cathedral. The 17th and 18th centuries saw the English king establish shipyards and ports to fight the Dutch and French. During Colgate's early childhood, Kent's coastline was also home to many smugglers, wars, and domestic resistance. During this chaotic period, Prime Minister William Pitt the Younger, who grew up in Kent, sent a secret message to William's father telling him he had only a few weeks to leave Britain forever or be arrested for his outspoken support of the French Revolution. As a yeoman, Robert was a freeholder and leader in the county as an official of the king. Still, he also upheld the county tradition of resisting government authority and speaking prominently for all freedom movements, including the American and French revolutions, which forced him to flee the island when William was twelve years old in 1795.

Moving a large young family across the ocean in a hurry created considerable hardship. The family moved first to Maryland, where Robert experienced many business failures

---

[36] 100-44 BC

and lost the Maryland farm due to title fraud when William was sixteen. During their time in Maryland, William's first job was making soap and candles in Baltimore. He worked hard. Amazingly, William paid off all his father's debts and saved enough to purchase another farm in the wilderness area of Delaware County, New York, in less than a year. As the oldest child, William worked to support his mother, father, and six siblings—two brothers[37] and four sisters.

William turned down his first job offer of an assistant clerk, even though he desperately needed the money, because he said, "Anyone can assist a clerk; I want to learn how to work and earn a living for myself."

At age eighteen, William left the farm penniless with no friends or credit to seek his fortune in New York City and find a way to support his family by making soap. During his journey to New York City, a canal boat captain offered this advice: "Someone will soon be the leading soap maker in New York. You can be that person. But you must never lose sight of the fact that the soap you make has been given to you by God. Honor Him by sharing what you earn. Begin by tithing all you receive."

He took this advice to heart even though the small soap company failed after two years. He tithed his cash profits, and when he started his next company he made sure that his product always had the full measure customers paid for—with the highest quality—and that every customer was satisfied.

---

[37] His brothers became both successful businessmen and prominent churchmen.

By the time William was twenty-three, he had risen to manage the largest tallow-chandler business in the city: Slidel and Company. Perhaps fortunately, Slidel and Company hit a series of bad business trends, which caused the company to shut down two years later.

Then William opened his own soap retail business. This was William's philosophy:

- Provide superior customer service to win and retain customers, even if it sometimes cost him a loss.
- Ask friends to review every major transaction so he could benefit from their counsel, particularly in checking whether he had overlooked anything.
- Avoid litigation whenever he could.

By age twenty-eight, in 1811, he was worth five thousand dollars (a fairly large sum in those days). That same year, he married Mary Gilbert.

Renaissance Entrepreneur

Upon the eruption of war against Britain the following year, he dominated the soap business in America. He started a starch factory—which became one of the largest in the young nation. In 1820 he added a starch factory in Jersey City, New

Jersey, across the Hudson River from New York City. When the foreman of his Jersey City factory, who was also his partner, started a competing factory in Jersey City Colgate, he kept much of the business volume because of his reputation in treating customers so well.

Long before he became wealthy, William committed to tithing 10 percent of his income to charity. He was captivated by the Great Revival, then sweeping New York state, especially the Baptist preacher John M. Mason. William joined Mason's church and quickly became a deacon. As his wealth grew, William joined the now-famous Tabernacle church, contributing a large percentage of its initial start-up and building costs.

As the company expanded rapidly into other consumer products—becoming one of the largest consumer product companies in America—William steadily increased his charitable giving until he reached 50 percent of his substantial profits donated each year to charitable causes. These activities included turning around the struggling Madison College and building it into a major institution. After his death, the college was renamed—in his honor—Colgate University. He also was a founder and major donor to both the American Bible Society in 1818 and later the American and Foreign Bible Society. When denominational differences threatened splits in the American Bible Society, he helped members unite around several accurate translations and focus on sharing those Bibles throughout the nation.

His avid support of mission work extended from his city throughout the nation to many foreign lands. He and his wife generously donated to and volunteered with the Sunday School movement, which later grew the YMCA among other organizations. All eleven of their children were also known as pious Christians who put their faith into action in numerous ways, supporting many charitable causes.

One of the church controversies William was involved in reflected his desire to share the Gospel message of salvation with everyone. When states began to cut off government funding for churches in the post-revolutionary period, it was still common practice for churches to rent out designated pews to raise revenue. William insisted that anyone could sit anywhere they pleased, in hopes of reviving the perception of the church as open to all. After many years, William swayed enough people to discontinue this old practice throughout the city. He supported many evangelistic crusades in the city and organized prayer teams to pray for the new converts in their neighborhoods. In addition to all this, he supplied full support for several missionaries.

William also funded seminaries and argued in favor of better-educated ministers so more people could hear the accurate, clear word of God. Late in life, he looked at the example of Brown University in Rhode Island which aimed to provide Christian education, particularly for clergy. But Brown University had already lost its purpose by 1850. Therefore, William insisted on bringing the pure Biblical message to as many people as possible. He promoted the idea that colleges must include in their charters a firm commitment to the Christian creed that the trustees would enforce to avoid the institution speedily becoming a godless prize of some faction, sect, or interest group.

In addition to spiritual support, William and his family were involved in social challenges. Although he never served alcohol in his home and was a powerful supporter of the temperance movement, William would befriend drunks on the streets, trying to help them turn their lives around. He also frequently invited traveling Baptist ministers into his home for free food, lodging, and entertainment.

Although preferring to avoid involvement in government affairs, he accepted the appointment as treasurer of the New York City Fire Department. When the city suffered from an especially scandal-plagued corrupt regime, William advocated replacing the administration. However, he declined requests to run for mayor as the honest alternative. Since New York City was the primary source of manufactured goods imported from Europe, many southern slaveholders would visit the city to purchase them. William opposed slavery but kept cordial relations with southern slaveholders in hopes they would eventually realize that slavery contradicts God's Word.

Compassion and peacemaking were hallmarks of William's life. As a teenager, he harbored vindictive feelings for his father's creditors but realized these feelings were damaging him. After forgiving those creditors for their harsh treatment, William recognized that he was then free to develop a positive character and achieve greater things in life. His wife, who had come from a wealthy family who disowned her when she converted to William's Baptist denomination, was in full accord with her husband, even though their initial years of marriage were a considerable step down from her accustomed lifestyle. Gradually William's in-laws and many people throughout the city and the nation recognized his abilities as a peacemaker in both business and church affairs. He was noted as impatient about any denunciations, even against corrupt people. William was cheerful to his many guests and showed wide reading and wit. He was known for his generosity, cheerfulness, and sympathy for everyone he encountered throughout his adult life.

Business associates and family members noted that the more William gave away for charitable purposes, the more rapidly his wealth grew. Still, he taught his family frugality. Even when he eventually could afford luxuries such as a private carriage, he walked everywhere because he believed a carriage would cut down the amount available for charity. Mary formed a women's Sunday School—one of the forerunners of the Sunday School Movement. She also raised funds along with her husband and granted endowed scholarships for students.

William Colgate lived out the Biblical wisdom he was given to "never lose sight of the fact that the soap you make has been given to you by God. Honor Him by sharing what you earn. Begin by tithing all you receive." And God blessed his efforts beyond all he could have imagined.

8

Accountability, Abolition, and Silk

"We will persevere,
come life or death"
— Lewis Tappan

The Tappan Brothers

1786-1865 & 1788-1873

Kindness towards all is not the only route to becoming a Christian tycoon. The Tappan brothers built a business empire upon the concept of societal accountability. In some cases, they risked their lives to call others to moral and financial accountability for their actions.

Transforming Accountability

The Tappan brothers were born in Northampton, Massachusetts. At the age of twenty-one, Arthur moved to Portland, Maine when it was still a Massachusetts department rather than a state, to start a dry goods store. After achieving modest success, Arthur, now joined by his brother Lewis, left the fairly new state of Maine to open a silk importing business in New York City in 1826. This enterprise rapidly became enormously profitable, although the unique challenge of who to trust became an increasing liability concern. International business was somewhat rare, especially for small business owners.

New York City was a major importer of manufactured goods from around the world and attracted customers from throughout America. These customers included the prosperous slave-holding plantation owners of the South, whose cotton crops could either afford them many luxury goods or cause them to default due to poor conditions or price changes.

Trust was a two-way street. The brothers were asked to extend credit to customers who may or may not pay months later when their crops were harvested. But the brothers also asked for credit from merchants and Chinese tradesmen—on the far side of the planet where the silk was spun. These Chinese merchants had their own problems, including frequent rebellions, rapid population growth, famines, and England's threats over whether to open up trade with the West using unequal treaty terms. All of these situations made Chinese merchants wary of extending much credit to Westerners.

Despite these credit or trust challenges, the Tappan brothers' silk business prospered into one of the richest in the city. They would always pay all their debts on time and they were widely known for their integrity and Bible-based reason. The year after they started their silk import business, the Tappan brothers along with Samuel Morse[38] founded New York Journal of Commerce, a business intelligence newspaper still published today. The Journal operated two deepwater schooners to intercept arriving vessels to get the stories ahead of all competition. After Morse invented the telegraph, the Journal became a founding member of a startup news network known as the Associated Press—still in operation today as the world's largest news-gathering organization.

Slavery and the Abolition Movement

The brothers insisted that the paper take an abolitionist position in the fight against slavery. However, Morse defended slavery and wanted to prohibit Catholics from holding public office. The brothers disagreed strongly with Morse's position on the matter. In response, they purchased his interest in the venture and admitted two new partners who were vehemently anti-slavery.

---

[38] 1791-1872. He invented both the telegraph and morse code system just a few years later.

Alongside the abolitionist position the paper took, the Tappan brothers prohibited immoral advertising, banning immoral ads in their paper. Coupled together, this stance on slavery and morality was controversial in New York City. But they believed God would prosper their publication as long as they were faithful to biblical principles in their businesses.

Nevertheless, it was an uphill battle. The history of slavery in New York City was intricately woven into the fabric of the city. Slavery began there under the Dutch, in 1626 when the city was still termed "New Amsterdam." The British expanded the practice of slavery to the point that by 1703, more than 42% of city households held slaves.[39]

The New York Manumission Society, founded in 1785, caused Southern states to urge the new national capital to be built in the south in 1790. The New York state legislature eventually passed a law in 1799 for the gradual abolition of slavery. However, the last New York slave was not set free until 1827. It was in this context, therefore, that the Tappan brothers started their newspaper.

With slavery in New York City well alive in recent memory, the economic effects of its abolition in that same city were yet to be fully realized. Much of the city's prosperity was linked to the spending habits of Southern plantation owners, who would not take kindly to the newfound freedom of New York's formerly enslaved residents. Abolition was harshly opposed.

---

[39] So many slaves were held by New-Yorkers that periodic slave revolts were of grave concern to the free residents.

Across the pond in England, the great abolitionist William Wilberforce[40] was hard at work. However, it would be six years before Britain became the first nation in world history to abolish slavery. William Wilberforce pushed hard for both the abolition of slavery and the general improvement of morals as his life's goal. He would succeed in aiding the abolition of the slave trade throughout nearly all of the British empire in 1833.[41] The movement, however, was not simply contained to England. The growing abolitionist sentiment in the United States and abroad greatly disturbed pro-slavery Americans, who feared a popular movement would accomplish the same result in the United States as it eventually would in England and the British Empire.

Arthur and Lewis continued their substantial funding and out-spoken support for reforming social ills by giving generously in both money and publicity to the American Bible Society, various church missions, and funding much of evangelist Charles G. Finney's Second Great Awakening Movement. The brothers received ridicule from their support for a campaign to end prostitution in New York and cease Sunday mail delivery to support a day of rest for everyone. They also gave substantial sums to Oberlin College in Ohio, one of the very few colleges at that time which took the highly controversial stance of admitting women and blacks as students. They also supported William Lloyd Garrison's newspaper *The Liberator*, which called for immediate abolition nationwide without compensation to slaveholders. It also insisted white people treat black

---

[40] 1759-1833

[41] The only nation in world history to do so up to that time!

people as equals in all areas of life—equals made in God's image, according to God's Word in Genesis.

The brothers' efforts to reform morals and especially eliminate slavery in America generated very harsh reactions. Both men's homes were sacked in the 1834 New York City anti-abolitionist riots. The pro-slavery mob raided Lewis's home to burn all his furniture in the street.

A few years later came The Panic of 1837. New York City banks dishonored specie (paper money) redemptions for gold causing a national depression that lasted until 1844. Rather than default on their obligations as many other merchants were doing and unable to get their own money out of their bank for a time, the brothers chose the more honorable course of simply closing their silk business. Although the business, as one of the largest in the nation, had been earning one million dollars in profit annually, its closure left a debt of 1.1 million dollars.[42] The brothers gave notes for six months, paying every cent they promised to on time.

Despite these personal and business setbacks, Arthur and Lewis felt led by God to continue speaking out against slavery. They quite vocally supported the abused Africans in the famous Amistad Supreme Court case of 1838, where the illegally enslaved Africans were freed and returned to their native Africa. Two years later, the brothers founded the American and Foreign Anti-slavery Society. They funded and widely distributed pamphlets explaining the Biblical proof that God

---

[42] Most Northeastern families, at this time, earned less than $400 per year.

opposed slavery. For these actions, denunciations of the brothers became common, and a mob in Charleston, South Carolina, made a bonfire of their pamphlets in 1835—while burning an effigy of Arthur high above the bonfire.

In 1841, the year after starting the anti-slavery society, the brothers formed the Mercantile Agency. This was the first credit rating agency in the entire world. The company provided credit rating reports of western businessmen—particularly plantation owners—for New York and Boston merchants. They also eventually expanded into rating the quality of many banks' notes. This was an era of many sudden bank failures and no national dollar currency or today's Federal Reserve. Lewis's well-known integrity and strict insistence for only Christian employees of the highest character built the firm's reputation into the most trusted company in America, despite the anger Southerners and New York merchants felt toward his stance on abolishing slavery.

Arthur and Lewis opened branch offices throughout the country with partners who knew the local plantation owners, bankers, and area merchants. These partners ran each local branch and shared in the national profits. Lawyers began submitting reports about merchants, plantation owners, and other business people they had to sue or who lived up to their obligations. This allowed Lewis, the managing partner of the Mercantile Agency, to develop a complete and detailed assessment of their creditworthiness. Merchants throughout the nation and abroad paid to review his books, ledgers, and notes so they could determine whether to issue trade credit. The reference book of 1859 began issuing ratings for companies and banks throughout the United States, Canada, and England. The brothers' vocal opposition to the Fugitive Slave Act of 1850 and the infamous Dred Scott Supreme Court case of 1858 miraculously did not hurt the ability of the credit agency to talk with pro-slavery people or gather business intelligence.

As the slavery debate in America continued to heat up and angry Southerners talked more openly about succession, the Tappan brothers decided to sell their Mercantile Agency to two former employees, Robert Dun and John Bradstreet. The former clerks renamed the Tappan brothers' partnership after themselves—Dun and Bradstreet. The Tappan brothers had started the credit rating industry, and their published ratings book and papers became today's Wall Street Journal.

During the Civil War, the Tappan brothers and their partners in the New York Journal of Commerce became so outspoken for the rights of black Americans that the Lincoln administration suspended their publication for three years. The brothers criticized how slow the government officials were to recognize the God-given rights of black people. So, the administration was fearful that the brothers would cause more rioting in New York City and undermine government support. From the 1830s through the 1860s, both brothers' houses were sacked several times by angry anti-abolition mobs. During the war, Lewis financially supported *The Emancipator* abolitionist newspaper and encouraged New York City churches to end the cultural practice of having separate seating areas for whites and blacks.

The brothers saw no false separation of church and commerce.

Their Journal of Commerce conveyed business and societal news from a Christian viewpoint. Lewis helped start the American Missionary Association to evangelize among all people, including blacks. The idea was to share the pure message of Jesus free from societal prejudices. In 1847 Lewis helped found the *National Era*, which in 1852 published Harriet Beecher Stowe's *Uncle Tom's Cabin*. This famous book, which many today—without reading it—wrongfully criticize as mocking blacks, in fact, pointed out the evils of slavery and galvanized an apathetic white public in the North to strongly oppose slavery.

Arthur's and Lewis's Biblical faith was the basis of their determination to see all black Americans free and treated as equal in God's sight by the American government. Bertram Wyatt-Brown's book on Lewis Tappan entitled *Lewis Tappan and the Evangelical War Against Slavery*[43] explains the inseparable Bible-based beliefs which caused the Tappan brothers to fight so fiercely for abolition and other social reforms. Interestingly, towards the end of his life, Lewis published the pamphlet entitled *Is It Right to be Rich?*[44] for other rich people. He concluded that while God may grant some people great prosperity, the purpose is not for personal pleasure but rather to relieve the suffering of others and bring the joy of the Gospel to them for both temporal and eternal benefit. Therefore, the rich person should endeavor to invest all his or her fortune in eternity, rather than in the earthly treasures which future generations might squander. That's exactly what the Tappan

---

[43] 1969

[44] 1869

brothers did.

9

Advertising, Sharing the Bounty, and Reapers

*"Indomitable perseverance in a business,
properly understood, always ensures ultimate success."*
— *Cyrus McCormick*

Cyrus McCormick

1809-1884

Even though they share the same core religious beliefs, Christians may often have differing political opinions and can be influenced by divergent cultural upbringings. For Cyrus McCormick, Southern roots affected him throughout his life. His upbringing on a family farm in Virginia instilled in him an appreciation for sharing the harvest in more ways than one.

Cyrus's father, Robert, was a failed inventor who worked many years to develop a mechanical reaper. Cyrus continued his father's work and received a patent, but his early 1831 design was considered too unreliable for local farmers. He could not sell more than a single reaper for the next ten years. During this period he worked in a blacksmith shop and metal smelting business with his brothers.

Despite their hard work, the Panic of 1837 nearly caused the family to go bankrupt. Still, Cyrus continued to improve his design. Finally, his efforts began to pay off when he sold reapers made in the family farm shop and received a second patent in 1845.

Sales started with just seven reapers in 1842, climbing to twenty-nine the next year, and soaring to fifty the year after that. Word spread about his invention. Cyrus noticed an increasing number of orders arriving from the Midwest where farms tended to be much larger and the land flatter, significantly improving the machine's reliability. As sales grew, he contracted with a New York company to manufacture the reapers, but poor product quality hurt his reputation.

In 1847 after their father's death, Cyrus and one of his brothers, Leander, moved to Chicago to establish a factory for mass production of his reapers. At the time, Chicago had no paved streets and was much less developed than other Midwestern cities. However, it had excellent water transportation for raw materials and railroad connections to the farther west—where most of the customers would be.

In 1848, Cyrus tried to renew his patent, but another inventor had filed a rival patent application only three months before him, which caused Cyrus delays and additional costs. In

1849, another brother, William, moved to Chicago to manage the company's financial affairs. Once his brother was based in Chicago, the company grew rapidly. While the reaper design helped, the primary reasons for this rapid growth were innovative sales and logistics expertise.

Transforming Marketing

Cyrus developed standardized marketing and sales techniques. He used these to train a vast network of salesmen to demonstrate machine operation in the field and obtain replacement parts quickly. Salesmen were even trained to repair machines in the field if necessary during crucial harvest times in the farm year. Company advertising—which was becoming a new industry at that time—built broad exposure and sales leads.

Cyrus faced many challenges as his business grew. An increasing number of competitors and patent challenges forced Cyrus to become more aggressive with his advertising and sales staff training. By 1856, the factory produced more than 4,000 reapers per year, primarily sold in the Midwest and West. Two years later, he married his secretary Nancy, affectionately called "Nettie," later in life, at the age of forty-nine.[45] When his factory burned down in the 1871 Great Chicago Fire and his health was declining, Cyrus considered closing the company, but Nettie urged him to rebuild it. When it reopened two years later, Nettie took on more in the family business to assist her ailing husband. She also became more involved in their

---

[45] The happy couple had seven children.

philanthropic affairs. The reaper business boomed to new heights with the new factory.

Cyrus was a very opinionated and stubborn man and a life-long active participant in Democrat Party politics, including supporting slavery. As a copperhead, the Civil War upset him greatly. During that era, a Copperhead was a northern Democrat who was pro-union but did not see anything wrong with guaranteeing southern slavery to keep the union together.

Sharing the Bounty

Despite his flaws, Cyrus was a committed Christian. After the war, he helped many former Confederate soldiers who were impoverished or disabled. As soon as he earned his first million dollars, Cyrus began funding a new seminary to train Presbyterian ministers. He was opposed to the drift away from recognizing the Bible as God's inherent Word, and thus diluting the impact of its improvement in individual's lives. He utilized his company profits throughout the years to fund primarily colleges and seminaries, as well as other religious and social needs.

The reaper saved farm labor and greatly boosted crop productivity, making farmers' lives much more prosperous. Most farm families had previously survived at barely more than a subsistence level. Cyrus believed his God-given mission in life was to feed the world through the improved bounty generated by his reapers. He endowed four professorships and was the major benefactor for the Theological Seminary of the

Northwest, which later was renamed McCormick Theological Seminary after his death.

In 1869, to further help those who were hurting, he donated ten thousand dollars to Dwight L. Moody.[46] With that money, he helped to reinstitute the Young Men's Christian Association (YMCA) in Chicago, which had financial difficulties due to the huge demand from poor people for rooms, food, Christian education, and wholesome recreational environments. His son Cyrus Jr. became the first president of the Moody Bible Institute.

Cyrus donated substantial sums to Tusculum College in Tennessee—and Nettie continued donations after his death. They also provided funding and support to establish churches and Sunday Schools in the South after the Civil War, regardless of the fact that Southern farmers were slow to adopt his farm machinery line and improved productivity practices.

Cyrus was also heavily involved in newspapers. He was a part-owner in the Chicago Times—later renamed the Chicago Herald—a Democrat Party pro-slavery newspaper. However, his views were unpopular with Illinois residents. Cyrus also purchased a religious newspaper, the *Interior*, which he renamed the *Continent* and built into a leading Presbyterian periodical.

While a prominent leader in the Democratic Party most of his life, his main societal interest was in promoting the

---

[46] 1837-1900

Christian message. He eventually became the largest donor to the Presbyterian church nationally, which Nettie continued after his death. For the last twenty years of his life, he was a major benefactor and trustee for Washington and Lee University in his native Virginia. In the last four years of his life, a stroke paralyzed his legs. Still, Cyrus and Nettie continued to fund many charitable causes and help those hurting from difficult circumstances. After his death, Nettie continued their Christian charitable efforts throughout the United States and abroad, donating over eight million dollars to hospitals, disaster and relief agencies, churches, youth organizations, educational institutions, and their Presbyterian denomination.

We can still observe Cyrus's legacy today. At a time when en-trepreneurs were not concerned about worker compensation, his son and grandson, who ran the company after his death, responded to a worker revolt, called the Haymarket riots.[47] Workers were striking citywide for an eight-hour day when anarchists threw a bomb into the crowd of workers, killing both workers and police officers. This was the beginning of the international socialist labor day known as May Day. Cyrus' son and grandson responded differently than other business owners. They collaborated with J.P. Morgan to create the better capitalized International Harvester Corporation in 1902. This corporation succeeded the old McCormick company and allowed the firm to boost productivity and afford higher wages for employees.

---

[47] 1886

82

By the time of Cyrus's death, his inventions had increased farm productivity while reducing the amount of back-breaking labor in thirty-six nations. This contributed significantly to the industrialization of agriculture and a related migration of labor to cities with increasing opportunities for better-paying jobs. The French Academy of Sciences elected him a corresponding member in 1878 for "having done more for the cause of agriculture than any other living man." The family donated the original Virginia farm to Virginia Tech, which operates the main property as a free museum and other sections as an experimental farm. He was also awarded numerous prizes and medals for his labor-saving and productivity-boosting reaper during his lifetime.

Cyrus' descendants continued to personally run the company until 2006, carrying on his tradition of charity. Thus, Cyrus fulfilled his calling to boost the food bounty for many people, the financial bounty for employees, customers, and vendors, and the spiritual bounty for the many people receiving his charitable efforts to share the Gospel.

10

Education and Social Entrepreneurship Amidst War

"It is better to set ten men to work
than to do the work of ten men."
Dwight Moody

Dwight Moody

1837-1900

Like a couple of our previous entrepreneurs, Dwight Moody also became heavily involved in education. However, he was more personally involved. He is also an excellent example of how Christian entrepreneurs can utilize the non-profit corporation route rather than the for-profit approach. This is often referred to today as social entrepreneurship.

Dwight L. Moody's father died when he was four, and his fifteen-year-old brother ran away shortly afterward, leaving his mother to support nine children by herself. Creditors seized his father's Northfield, Massachusetts business assets, leaving his mother destitute. What a severe beginning!

To her credit, his mother managed to support the children—though just barely—and, most importantly, give them a solid understanding of God's Word and church involvement. Eventually, his mother had to send off her children to work for their room and board, so Dwight was apprenticed to a local businessman. When he turned seventeen, Dwight moved to Boston to work in his uncle's shoe store. One of his uncle's requirements was that he regularly attended church.

A Transformed Life

In April 1855, at the age of nineteen, Dwight was converted to evangelical Christianity when his Sunday school teacher, Edward Kimball, talked to him about how much God loved him. Mr. Kimball wrote in his comment on Dwight's church membership application:

> *I can truly say, and in saying it I magnify the infinite grace of God as bestowed upon him, that I have seen few persons whose minds were spiritually darker than was his when he came into my Sunday School class; and I think that the committee of the Mount Vernon Church seldom met an applicant for membership more unlikely ever to become a Christian of clear and decided views of Gospel truth, still less to fill any extended sphere of*

public usefulness.

That conversion sparked the start of his evangelist career.

Later that year, Dwight traveled west to seek his fortune in Chicago as a shoe salesman, a job in which he was very successful. Dwight, a descendant on both sides from the original Puritan settlers, had no formal education. Still, he possessed a strong desire to share the Gospel, especially with the poorest and most reprobate.

By day, he was a shoe salesman. By night, he frequented the "Sands" area of Chicago, noted for saloons and prostitution, where he started a small Sunday School in the heart of immense human misery. During the great 1857-1858 Christian revival in Chicago, Dwight was involved in turning around the financially floundering YMCA in Chicago to meet the rapidly growing needs of the poor in the city.

One observer noted that Dwight started in an old abandoned saloon shanty. He struggled to read Bible stories to local residents of all races and circumstances. Due to his tireless labor, average attendance increased to 650, with sixty volunteers from various churches serving as teachers, within a year. His Sunday school became so well known that in 1860 President-elect Abraham Lincoln visited and spoke at Dwight's Sunday school class in the Sands ghetto.

Transforming Communities with Nonprofit Education

When the Civil War started Dwight convinced Emma Dryer[48], principal, and teacher at Illinois State Normal University, to continue his work in the slums of Chicago. Dryer also started a training school for young women. Thus, Emma continued Dwight's work in Chicago while he assisted in ministry for the soldiers of war.

Although Dwight could not bring himself to enlist when the Civil War started due to his religious objections against harming others, he found other ways to assist in the war. Following the horrors of the first battle at Bull Run, the national YMCA organization formed the United States Christian Commission (USCC) to supply food, clothing, medical supplies, recreation, religious literature, chaplains, and nurses to the Union soldiers at or near the battlefronts.

Dwight volunteered for the USCC and helped at nine visits to battlefields, including the brutal Battle of Shiloh and the bloody Wilderness campaign that allowed Dwight to accompany General Grant's troops into Richmond at the fall of the Confederacy. During the war, in 1862, he married Emma Revel, a worker at his Sunday school.

Dwight met Ira D. Sankey at a YMCA convention in 1870. Ira was a Union soldier who worked as an IRS agent after the war. Several months after they met, Ira attended his first

---

[48] 1835-1925

evangelistic meeting with Dwight, causing Ira to resign his government position to join Dwight's staff and become one of the most prominent hymn writers and singers of the 19th century. Dwight and Ira became good friends.

On Sunday, October 8, 1871, while Ira and Dwight were in the middle of an evangelistic meeting in the Sands, the Great Chicago Fire broke out, killing 300 people, destroying 3.3 square miles,[49] and leaving over 100,000 residents homeless and destitute. The fire lasted two full days. Dwight himself reported that he "saved nothing but his reputation and his Bible."

By this time, Dwight had become famous across America. A wealthy Chicago supporter offered to build him a new house to persuade Dwight to stay in Chicago. Supporters in New York, Philadelphia, and elsewhere were making the same offer. Instead, he chose to purchase the farm next door to his birthplace in Northfield, Massachusetts. Dwight felt he could recover faster from his preaching tours in a tranquil setting.

During this period in his life, as he conducted evangelism meetings throughout America, he also organized summer conferences led and attended by prominent Christian preachers and evangelists worldwide. He established two schools—the Northfield School for Girls[50] and the Mount Hermon School

---

[49] Especially the poorer area where they were preaching.

[50] 1879

for Boys,[51] which later merged into today's co-educational Northfield Mount Hermon School.

Early in 1886, Dwight and several Chicago residents formed the Chicago Evangelization Society. Dwight noticed it was difficult to find qualified Christians to counsel all the many new converts who had numerous questions about the faith and how to begin living a Christ-like lifestyle. He organized classes that grew into degree programs and a seminary. During the first ten years, the Society graduated over 10,000 students to enter the mission fields throughout America and worldwide.

Although he no longer lived in Chicago, Dwight continued visiting the city and supervising his ministry there. He continued to be personally active until a month before his death. For example, the Columbian Exposition[52] proved to be an excellent opportunity to rapidly expand the ministry worldwide. Larger businesses nationwide took turns paying the daily rent for evangelism meetings, and smaller ones covered administrative and personnel expenses.

During a trip to the United Kingdom in 1872, Dwight became well known in Europe for his evangelistic efforts. He preached almost a hundred times, filling many stadiums, including the Botanic Gardens Palace—which had an audience upward of 30,000 people. When he returned to the United States, crowds of 12,000 to 20,000 were as common as they had been in the United Kingdom. President Grant and some of his cabinet

---

[51] 1881

[52] Also referred to as the 1893 Chicago World's Fair.

attended a meeting in January 1876.

Dwight utilized a cross-cultural book called *The Wordless Book* invented by the famous pastor Charles Spurgeon,[53] whom Dwight met during his British evangelism tour. This book is still used to teach the Gospel message to many illiterate people worldwide. During the UK tour, Dwight raised £10,000 to build a new home for the Carrubbers Close Mission, an evangelism outreach center for the Edinburgh, Scotland area.

Dwight was a physically large man and an enthusiastic and caring evangelist. His style could be brusque, but he always showed he cared. His final campaign in Kansas City filled a new four-floor auditorium with 20,000 people eager to hear his message. He was a social entrepreneur.[54] He knew how to utilize leverage as a key planning concept in all his schools and evangelistic organizations. He stated multiple times, "It is better to set ten men to work than to do the work of ten men." All his work and schools were for laity, so they could reach the lost where no clergy might be able to reach.

In the year of his death, the board renamed the organization the Moody Bible Institute. It also expanded to offer formal programs of study both in person and via correspondence for those who could not afford to travel to Chicago. Dwight's legacy continues well beyond the grave, with his Massachusetts and Chicago schools thriving today and the

---

[53] 1834-1892

[54] Someone who creates new organizations for societal enrichment rather than monetary profit.

graduates sharing the Good News of Jesus throughout the world.

11

Affordability, Generosity, and Wood Barrels

"Gain all you can, save all you can, and give all you can."
—John Wesley

John D. Rockefeller

1839-1937

Sometimes God employs tough-minded efficiency experts to bring dramatically greater prosperity to countless people. Some non-Christians have argued that such a person is a "robber baron." Others disagree. You can read the facts of this story and judge for yourself. Regardless, one thing is indisputable: God worked through a hard-driving man to improve efficiency in a way that continues to make life more affordable and mission work more effective.

John Davison Rockefeller Sr. was the wealthiest person in the world at the time, which may be why so many socialists disparage him and call him a "Robber Baron." However, he started life destitute. Every cent he accumulated was voluntarily given to him by customers who were grateful for all the money he saved them.

John was born into a large family in rural northern New York. His mother was devoutly religious, but his father was a con man. His father would frequently abandon the family for months at a time—causing them to move often. Eventually, the family settled in Cleveland, Ohio, where John became an assistant bookkeeper at age sixteen.

By the age of twenty, he and three partners launched a produce business. The business prospered modestly to the point where John and his brother William[55] along with another investor, Samuel Andrews,[56] bought out the other three original partners and formed Rockefeller & Andrews, becoming a commissioned grain merchant. However, in the mid-1860s, Cleveland had become an oil boomtown. John left the grain business to start his own oil refinery. In 1867, Henry Flagler[57] provided much-needed one hundred thousand dollars of capital and became a partner in Rockefeller, Andrews & Flagler.

Henry managed the grain side of the business. Using his network of contacts, Henry developed the idea of providing rebates to large volume purchasers. This enabled the young company to undercut all competition pricing. Starting around

---

[55] 1841-1922

[56] 1836-1904

[57] 1830-1913

the end of the Civil War, Cleveland grew from a rough frontier town into a center for the oil industry.

John noticed the high risk taken by "wildcatters"[58] and how often they failed. Yet petroleum was becoming an affordable alternative to the more expensive whale oil for lamp lighting. John decided the new petroleum industry's refining end offered much more stable profit opportunities—leaving the high-risk drilling gambles to others. The company prospered and immediately recycled nearly all profits into purchasing more local refineries. Railroads were also beginning to convert to the cheaper petroleum to use as lubrication. By 1870 the company required reorganization from a partnership into a corporation. They named it Standard Oil Company, Inc.

The new corporation expanded from refining kerosene and gasoline for lighting purposes into transportation and marketing. Very quickly, it became the largest oil refinery in the world. The company built a horizontal integration. It controlled many refineries in the general areas near major oil well drilling operations.

Even during this period, John struggled with ethical choices that face a successful, revenue-generating business created for the entrepreneur. The belief in God that John's mother had taught him caused him to feel queasy about buying his way out of serving in the Union Army during the Civil War. This was a legally acceptable option for those who could afford it, and John justified his action by saying he was supplying food to

---

[58] Small companies who drill wells hoping to find oil.

the troops—plus, if he left his new business, it would collapse.

Henry, who was the son of a minister, did not have the same concerns about avoiding the draft. But after the war, both men supported the church and charitable efforts to share the Bible with the increasing number of people moving to the Cleveland area as their version of their war effort. Through the business-building phase of his life, John attended church regularly.

He also got married. He met his wife, Laura Celestia Spelman,[59] during an accounting class. She was an abolitionist, active in politics, and a volunteer in the Underground Railroad helping escaped slaves secure their freedom. During the war, she returned to her native Massachusetts to become a teacher before returning to Ohio to teach. Laura and John were married in 1864. They had five children.

Laura and John tithed faithfully throughout their marriage. In addition to her devotion to her children, Laura was also devoted to philanthropy. She gave generously to Atlanta Baptist Female Seminary in Atlanta, founded in 1881 to provide a college education for newly freed black female slaves. The school's founders met John at a church conference. He decided to visit the school and was so impressed with their progress that he paid the school's entire debt. Laura began giving such large amounts that only a few years after its founding, school officials changed the name to its present name in 1884—Spelman College—in her honor.

---

[59] 1839–1915

Transforming Affordability

During these years, Standard Oil rapidly grew to control 90 percent of all oil refining in the United States and became one of the few international corporations of that era. His company's first big threat came from Thomas Edison[60] demonstrating his new incandescent light bulb in 1879. Edison declared, "We will make electricity so cheap that only the rich will burn candles." Until that time, John's major source of wealth had been supplying cleaner-burning, cheaper, and less smelly kerosene for lighting to replace whale oil. Now electric grids threatened to displace his oil lighting sales with competitive, no-smell electricity that could also fuel other machinery in the home and factory.

Fortunately for John and Standard Oil Company, new discoveries created a much greater demand for his products than he lost, particularly for gasoline. In the 1890s, Rudolf Diesel[61] invented an efficient internal combustion engine. Around this same time, Henry Ford[62] launched Ford Motor Company in 1903 as the car manufacturer who most efficiently and effectively built cars so low cost that any middle-class family could afford to buy one. His cars ran on gasoline, as did most other car manufacturers.

By the early 1900s, John had provided the same benefit to the transportation industry as he had done earlier to the lighting

---

[60] 1847-1931

[61] 1858-1913

[62] 1863-1947

industry, driving the cost of fuel down by an astonishing 99 percent. The result was an explosion of freedom for families to travel for leisure or move more easily to where many new jobs were being created. The unintended consequences of that drive downward in the price of fuel had other benefits. Much of the drop in transportation costs were passed onto customers in lower prices on products. Larger companies could afford to continue dropping prices as competition became more intense due to the increased ability to build large networks of offices and warehouses around the nation, thanks to lower transport costs.

Save All You Can

John was thrifty. Early in his career, most oil producers kept about 60 percent of the oil to produce kerosene but dumped the other 40 percent of sludge to create environmental disasters. John used the 40 percent—refining it into gasoline to run his factories and selling the rest as lubricating oil, petroleum jelly, and paraffin wax. Tar was used for paving, and naphtha was sent to gas plants. He hired his own plumbers rather than follow industry practice to subcontract the work. As a result, he cut the cost of pipe-laying in half.

John purchased wood and had employees build barrels, dropping his cost from $2.50 to $0.96 per barrel. He heavily borrowed whenever he saw bargain acquisition or expansion opportunities, reinvesting nearly all profits, adapted rapidly to changing markets, and hired marketing detectives to track changes in market conditions. Though he was a tough competitor, he saw himself as "an angel of mercy"—absorbing the weak competition to make the entire industry stronger, more efficient, and more competitive. He relentlessly drove prices downward to increase market share, stave off competitors, and help make products more affordable by developing over 300 types of oil-based products. He used his early bookkeeping experience to figure out how to organize operations more efficiently.

Many people branded him as stingy with worker wages because of his cost-cutting strategies. However, he paid the prevailing market rate, although when market demand dropped, he was equally quick to fire employees until market demand improved. Fundamentally, he attempted to balance a free market economics conception of market demand with his Christian beliefs of charity.

Market Opportunities & Innovation

But his economic savviness did not stop there. John understood that pipelines were a cheaper alternative to using railroads, and innovated accordingly. In 1877 the Pennsylvania Railroad, Standard Oil's primarily hauler, tried to purchase oil refineries in an attempt to block John and force him to give up his ability to demand reductions and rebates on railroad hauling charges. Standard Oil countered by holding back shipments and working with other railroads. The result was a freight war that lowered the cost of goods for all American families nationwide. In 1884 he moved the company to New York from Ohio, helping create a significant boost to the New

York City economy, and permanently connecting his name to NYC as a titan of industry.

As market share gradually eroded during the late 1880s, John developed an innovation by selling certificates to speculators for oil in his pipelines and storage facilities. He thus created the first oil futures market, allowing more stable and predictable oil prices. Connecting the new oil futures spot market with the financial markets helped stabilize and drive down oil-related prices such as gasoline and kerosene even further. This assisted other industries to likewise prevent wild price swings and bring an ever-increasing plethora of products within affordable reach of the average person. During this maturing phase of his business, John created over 100,000 jobs.

By 1911 John was worth approximately 2 percent of America's entire economy—an effective monopoly of the American economy. This was the year the government decided to attack and dismember his Standard Oil Company. By this time Henry had left the company, although he remained on the board of directors. In 1888, after the death of Henry's first wife and marriage to his second wife, he moved to Florida. There he became the largest developer in Florida history, completing a railroad along the entire eastern coast of Florida all the way to Key West by 1912. Unfortunately, these development projects in a far-off state meant John did not have the frequent advice of his old friend Henry during the government lawsuits against his company.

John's organizational structure had evolved to provide strong incentives and profit-sharing with regional partners. He created the business trust concept. Shareholders in acquired refineries or companies placed their stock in a trust along with John's Standard Oil stock. The stockholders became beneficiaries in the trust and had some voting rights. The effect became like a trade association or group of interrelated companies working together with a common direction. Effectively, they operated as a parent company—subsidiary holdings model.

The Standard Oil Trust ended up completely owning fourteen corporations and exercising majority control over twenty-six others. Nine individuals holding trust certificates acted as the trust's board of trustees, with John owning 41 percent of the trust certificates. Now the company pursued vertical as well as horizontal integration of business operations. Vertical integration involves the entire process from oil discovery and drilling to transport, refining, production, storage, wholesale marketing, and retail sales outlets. The retail sales outlets became known as gas stations.

Some people began to fear John had gained monopoly control over an increasingly vital fuel source. This led to passage by Congress of the 1890 Sherman Antitrust Act—the law under which the federal government sued Standard Oil in 1911. The judge ordered Standard Oil to be broken up into thirty-four separate companies, most of whom are still operating today, such as ExxonMobil, Chevron, etc. Eleven were allowed to keep the Standard Oil moniker as part of their name. John kept stock in all of these companies, but eventually sold most of it as he began to withdraw from business endeavors. Ironically, the primary effect of the breakup was to release more market value in the stock markets, tripling John's net worth and making him possibly the world's first billionaire.

Transforming Philanthropy

After losing his anti-trust lawsuit in 1911, John devoted the remaining four decades of his life to philanthropy. As this section demonstrates, his charitable works were intimately connected with his business operations, personal life, faith, and family. He created the modern systematic approach for targeted charity, forming foundations centered on medicine, education, and scientific research. Among the accomplishments he funded is the near eradication of hookworm and yellow fever in America.

He also left his mark on American education and medical research. He also founded the University of Chicago in 1890 through the American Baptist Education Society. He endowed Rockefeller University as a leading biomedical research university in 1901, considerably boosting the prestige of American medical science.

But his efforts did not stop there. Earlier, during the Spanish-American War, which resulted in Spain ceding the Philippines to America in 1898, John became interested in mission work to spread the Gospel message among Filipinos. The Presbyterian Union Mission Hospital was already operating in Iloilo when John brought the Presbyterian missionaries and the American Baptist Foreign Mission Society to plan and launch the Central Philippine University in 1905. It had two schools initially. One provided industrial training for boys. The other trained men to become pastors.

Throughout his life, John was a faithful member of Erie Street Baptist Mission Church. He taught Sunday school and served as a trustee, clerk, and sometimes janitor. He believed God was the guiding force to his success throughout his entire life. He stated that his mother strongly instilled in him these vital ethics: "From the beginning, I was trained to work, to save, and to give." He also followed Reverend John Wesley's advice to, "gain all you can, save all you can, and give all you can." John's charitable activity was not limited to his later years. From at least the time he left home to take his first job, and throughout the lean early years of building his business, John gave generously to many causes. When he married, his wife joined him. They were so committed to generosity that they even helped when they did not have extra money and had to sometimes borrow to do so.

John attended prayer meetings twice a week. At times, he donated tens of thousands of dollars to Christian groups while simultaneously borrowing over a million dollars to expand his business. He followed the principle in Luke 6:38 to "Give, and it will be given to you. Good measure, pressed down, shaken together, running over, will be put into your lap. For with the measure you use it will be measured back to you."

For his time, he was radically progressive on the issue of racial integration and racial equality. John was as ardent an abolitionist as his wife, but he expected proof that his donations were utilized efficiently and effectively. He was a big donor to both white and black Baptist churches throughout the South and other Christian denominations. One time an employee saw him pay for a slave's freedom. As a couple, they each worked towards the cause of equality and realizing the founding vision of America, that "all men are created equal"[63] as a principle enshrined not only in American law but also in Christian doctrine.

But if there was one thing he hated, it was waste. Not only did he optimize business operations, but he also invented the conditional grant as a means to assure more efficient charitable activities, holding charities accountable for achieving certain milestones within set time frames. These conditions were designed to find people in the institution who were personally concerned. In this way, he made sure he could count on them to cooperate and contribute.

John formed the General Education Board in 1903 to promote education at all levels throughout the nation. One of these projects led to starting the Rockefeller Sanitary Commission in 1909, which eradicated hookworm in the United States. John then created the Rockefeller Foundation in 1913 and funded it with a quarter of a billion-dollar donation (at a time when the average family earned 850 dollars per year) to expand upon the work of the Sanitary Commission, which was folded into the Foundation two years later.

The foundation focused on public health improvement, medical training, and the arts. Among other notable charity efforts,

---

63 U.S. Declaration of Independence.

the foundation started Johns Hopkins School of Hygiene and Public Health, the first such school of its kind. It also built the Peking Union Medical College in China and provided funding to medical schools and universities around the world. During World War I, John and his foundation provided significant relief for people harmed by the war.

The Laura Spelman Rockefeller Memorial Foundation was created in 1918. This foundation supported social studies to improve the lives of ordinary people. This foundation later merged into the Rockefeller Foundation. Throughout his lifetime, John gave away most of his fortune in keeping with his personal philosophy and Christian beliefs. His donations were estimated to exceed half a billion dollars.

And he practiced what he preached: equality, frugality, and efficiency. Later in life, John became well known for giving dimes to adults and nickels to children wherever he went during the Great Depression. During his working years in New York City, he insisted on commuting on public transportation despite multiple death threats. In retirement, he tended not to travel much but freely offered cash and advice to many people he met as he walked on the streets or rode on public transportation in New York City.

Biographer Allan Nevins described John as providing fair terms to competitors he bought out, often making them wealthy in a field so risky that few investors or entrepreneurs were willing to try it. He described John as

...more humane toward competitors than Carnegie; we

have the conclusion of another historian that his wealth was "the least tainted of all the great fortunes of his day."

The so-called Robber Barons, it should be remembered, improved the quality of life for most citizens. They did not use governmental coercion to force anyone to pay them. Instead, They made fortunes serving the needs of others first by creating many jobs and driving down prices so the majority of people could purchase items that had formerly been affordable only to the wealthy. In addition to all that, they gave away much of their fortunes to benefit many struggling individuals at a time when government welfare programs were nearly non-existent. And the fruits of their labors continue producing a more generous and more affordable world to this day.

12

Employee Care, Gospel through Education, and Horseradish

"We get out of life what we put into it."
— Henry Heinz

Henry Heinz

1844-1919

While still understanding the value of a dollar, some Christian entrepreneurs emphasized compassion for people. God offers many varied paths for faithful servant leaders to bring help and healing to a broken world. Our next entrepreneur story demonstrates how to transform the lives of not only his own employees but, by competitive example, the lives of everyone else's future employees.

Transforming the Food Industry

Henry Heinz, son of German Lutheran immigrants, was born in Pittsburgh, which had become one of America's largest cities by that time. His mother's piousness and frugality were major factors shaping his values. Henry began working with his mother in her garden as a young child, selling produce to local grocers as a kid. As a teenager, he harvested and sold horseradish, known for freshness and quality far beyond competitors. Unlike other food product companies at that time, he refused to bottle his products in dark glass jars. Instead, he used clear containers so customers could easily verify that his products were high quality.

Upon reaching age twenty-one (the legal age of adulthood back then), Henry used his modest savings from childhood vegetable sales to buy a half interest in his father's brick-making business. He then promptly added heating flues and drying apparatus to create brick-making capacity throughout the winter. This addition substantially boosted profits during the high-demand Spring building season. At age twenty-four, he formed a partnership with L.C. Noble to manufacture bricks in another nearby small Pennsylvania town. Henry made enough profit to build his father a new home and furnish it all before his father returned from a trip to Germany. He paid cash to avoid the mortgage.

He applied this philosophy of debt avoidance to both life and work. He took a cautious approach—testing products until he was sure all employees would produce only the highest possible quality. They would pay all bills immediately upon presentation, never asking for credit terms, since he couldn't tolerate debts.

Henry was exceptional in targeting the elimination of all waste in every task he tackled, whether large or small, in both resources and time. He instilled this hatred of waste in all his employees and suppliers. Noble joined him in starting a small food products company in 1869, which they ran out of the Heinz home. They began with selling the horseradish the family harvested in their garden. Then Henry bought crops from other farmers and gardeners, eventually expanding into offering pickles, vinegar, and other processed foods.

The Panic of 1873[64] caused many business owners to file for bankruptcy during the depression, but Henry survived. However, a bumper crop of unusually large size grew in 1875. In an attempt to keep his commitment to purchase all crops from his farmer-suppliers for their own growth in a national depression, Henry actually induced his own bankruptcy. Due to the banking and government mismanagement of the national currency and the money supply dropping to dangerous levels, banks refused to make any loans. Even credit-worthy customers such as Henry were denied loans. Although Henry tried to meet his promises and offered his personal assets as collateral, he was eventually forced to declare bankruptcy later that year.

His wife, Sarah, whom he married in 1869, supported and encouraged him to start anew, building on his reputation for

---

[64] It lasted until 1879.

high-quality products. Lacking the capital to start alone, he formed a company under the ownership of his cousin Frederick and his brother John. He then became the manager of this company—F&J Heinz.

Not only did Henry start again within months of his first company failing, but he dared to add a new product immediately:

Ketchup.

The new food products company provided the freshest products on the market plus an innovation not commonly found among businesses at that time—high customer service even after-sales. Other companies considered their obligations to respond to customers ended when the sale was completed. Henry, however, followed up to make sure customers' questions, concerns, and suggestions received responses.

He was considerate to solve customer's problems, and in the process transformed the food industry. To save homemakers the eye-stinging strain from cutting horseradish vegetables, Henry processed horseradish for people—developing the concept of packaged food. In this manner, he also developed another idea of building brand identity and brand loyalty, not merely promoting particular products.

In 1893, Henry rented a booth at the Columbian Exposition, also known as the Chicago World's Fair. Disappointed that few people walked up to his second-floor booth, he began offering a free pickle to entice them.[65] He even graciously helped his competitors attract more people to the second floor of the exhibition space using creative group advertising efforts. Within a few days, support beams had to be added to keep the floor from sagging under the weight of all the visitors seeking out his booth!

A few years later, in 1896, Henry developed the slogan "57 varieties" to use extensively in advertising, even though he had more than fifty-seven products by then. Later, when asked why he chose this number, he simply said he liked the number fifty-seven.

Raising the Bar for Business Ethics

Henry took morality in his business so seriously that he even kept a Moral Obligation Log, listing every creditor the bankruptcy judge discharged. Although he had no legal obligation to do so, and it was considered rare and odd to do this, Henry eventually paid back every cent of those discharged debts.

One creditor who tried to damage Henry's reputation and gave him many legal problems himself fell into financial difficulties several years later. When Henry heard the sheriff was selling this former creditor's house and furniture, he sent someone to bid the highest price to win his former tormentor's assets.

---

[65] This earned him the nickname Pickle King as pickle sales skyrocketed after then.

Then he presented them as a gift to the man's family so the sheriff could not seize them. The former creditor later heard that it was Henry who performed this anonymous act of charity. He thanked Henry profusely, telling him and others that while he treated Henry as an enemy, Henry turned out to be his only friend. This story was a typical example of how Henry used his modest but growing profits to care for others.

Henry eventually bought out his partners and incorporated the company in 1905, hiring some of his family to help run the firm. He treated all his employees as part of his Heinz Family, as he referred to them. He listened to ideas and concerns equally from directors and managers, factory employees, suppliers, customers, and even children in the neighborhood, who frequently would visit him at his office.

During the company's early years, Henry's church leaders challenged him to make a 200 dollars pledge to the congregation for ministry and charitable outreach to those suffering during the depression. At this time, the average American family earned $129 annually—less than fifty cents per workday. Henry wanted to help the disadvantaged, but he had absolutely no money at that time, as he was struggling to climb out of bankruptcy.

Because of his insistence on paying everyone in full and promptly and on the high quality of his products and business dealings, he was a member of a savings and loan association. The association would periodically have a lottery that offered to lend some of the increase in deposits at favorable loan rates. Thanks to God's will, Henry won the savings and loan lottery that year and promptly gave the loan proceeds to the church to fulfill his pledge. He believed God would always provide, so Henry should always strive to help others, even if he had nothing of his own to give.

He applied this belief of helping others to business. He strove to ensure that everyone won in every transaction he entered into. Henry would closely scrutinize every detail of the business and bargain hard for fair pricing. He applied this principle whether he was buying or selling with suppliers and customers alike, even if he had to borrow to pay more promptly than any other business or faster than the terms required. He stood firmly by his morals.

When he caught an employee acting immorally, his retribution was swift. He fired an employee on the spot for bragging that he had added an extra weight to a scale to save on paying for a load of produce. He also fired another employee who showed up drunk after having been warned the first time.

One employee's productivity and reliability had declined after his wife contracted a severe illness that required prolonged hospitalization. "Business is business, and charity is charity," he was known to say. He then ordered the manager to quietly pay for the former employee's wife's hospital visit and support his children until the wife was discharged from the hospital.

Transforming Employee Care

At one point, Henry offered raises to employees if they would always greet customers, vendors, and fellow employees with a smile. He coaxed employees to eliminate waste and improve efficiency continuously, rather than demanding or ordering that they do so. His management style was open and encouraging, which contrasted sharply with other entrepreneurs and managers of that era.

Henry also had other peculiar human resource ideas which stood out prominently from other businesses. He promoted from within the company—giving all employees hope of advancing as high as their talent and hard work could take them. He pioneered meetings of sales and other types of employees to network and share early "best practices" ideas between themselves. Henry invested substantial time teaching his ethical values to managers, so they absorbed them in their daily behavior and actively taught them to everyone below those managers. All of this created a strong, intentional corporate culture of excellence and highly Christian business ethics.

One of the results of this personnel approach was the H.J. Heinz Company never had unions or any labor disputes while he was alive and for many years afterward. It was a stark contrast to what was going on around him at that time. The famous Haymarket Square Riots[66] in Chicago was a bloody confrontation between police and labor union members. Throughout the

---

[66] May 4, 1886.

1880s, when working conditions were frequently dangerous and wages low, socialists and anarchists formed the labor movement to violently protest for better working conditions and salaries and dismantle the free enterprise system. Sympathetic journalists, called Muckrakers, wrote articles stirring up labor unrest among much of the general public. Henry, however, had no such labor troubles. His employees repeatedly said they were happy with his treatment as an employer.

One time, a union executive demanded the contractors for a factory he was building in another part of the country must use only union labor. Henry quickly agreed on the condition they review his own company carefully. If they found no employee discontent, the union officials would not attempt to unionize or to agitate laborers or the community against him, as they had begun to do. He gave them free access to all his employees at all of his factories throughout America. The union officials scrutinized every small detail of his entire operation for months. Still, they could find no fault with his labor relations.

Transforming Advertising with Generosity

Henry was also one of the first entrepreneurs to combine civic help with brand advertising. For example, he built the Heinz Ocean Pier in Atlantic City, New Jersey, for tourists to enjoy free concerts, free bathroom facilities (when nobody, even the local government, made this available), and art exhibitions as well as displays of his product line. He sponsored similar free recreational opportunities to the general public in other parts of the nation.

In 1886 he took his first three-month trip to Europe, visiting sites of Christian saints and their famous acts, yet also selling his products along the journey. He also took time to truly get to know local people, which became the basis of his company expanding internationally. He kept meticulous notes about many detailed observations of all he saw and heard during this trip, whether related to business, religious beliefs, political situations, and everything else.

Henry's financial giving was as generous as his sharing of his time and expertise. In addition to serving as a trustee for the University of Pittsburgh, he donated large amounts frequently for art, music, and education for the masses of people. But he was most passionate about spreading and strengthening the Christian faith so people might benefit permanently and eternally, not just temporarily on earth.

Spreading the Gospel Through Education

Henry gave abundantly to the International Sunday School movement. This vast movement began in 1780 in England and arrived in America during the War of 1812. It set up schools teaching both the Bible and secular topics[67] for needy children and adults at no cost. They met on Sundays since this was the one day of the week when workers had a day of rest and could attend. The schools were independent from

---

[67] Math, reading, history, etc.

churches, although many churches eventually incorporated such schools into their community services decades later. Keep in mind that while some communities in New England built free tax-supported schools as early as the 1630s, a statewide system of free public education did not arrive until Massachusetts implemented a "common school" model in the late 1830s. This idea gradually expanded southward and westward until all states supplied public education after the Civil War. However, today's comprehensive school day, school year, and curriculum goals were not achieved in some states until as late as the 1930s.

During Henry's lifetime, many people could not obtain an education and advance their opportunities. In Henry's era, the government-run schools were gradually crowding out these independent Sunday School movement schools from teaching secular subjects, so the schools moved towards focusing on Biblical education, even though the public schools of that era also taught the Bible and the Christian faith. In 1872 the Sunday School movement produced the International Uniform Lesson Series[68] to help teachers and students (both adults and children) in rural or poor areas to obtain more consistent and intellectually appropriate teaching. This series of lessons allowed people to learn at their level "from cribs to canes." By 1900—just before Henry's company had grown so large he had to incorporate and restructure it—the movement opened schools in many areas where there were few or no churches. Today this movement continues worldwide under several

---

[68] Governments eventually adopted this idea, referring to it as "grade" schools for grouping people with similar levels of learning achievements.

different names, bringing many millions of individuals to faith in Christ. Henry was one of many Christian entrepreneurs who funded the rapid growth of this movement.

Henry not only donated large sums of money, he personally helped conduct surveys of cities to canvas the unreached with the Gospel. His trip to Japan built strong relations between both nations. It started Sunday Schools to grow Christianity in Japan during a time when wary Japanese officials kept the country closed to most Western influence. For more than twenty years, he traveled every county in Pennsylvania, raising funds and promoting outreach for the Sunday School movement.

Henry's wife, Sarah—whom he called Sallie—was also well known throughout Pittsburgh for personally tending to the sick throughout their married life until she died. She ran many women's Bible studies, volunteered at the local hospital, and managed even more charitable activities around Pittsburgh (Henry endowed a Sunday School teacher program at the University of Pittsburgh.) and Sharpsburg. After twenty-five years of marriage, Sallie died in 1894.

Henry, who lived another twenty-five years but never remarried, cherished her in his heart. He built the Sarah Heinz building as a huge youth training and recreation center for the Pittsburgh area's poorest youth to give them a good start in life. Both of them spent time caring for and talking with the poor youth of the city. Henry often showed up late for business meetings because he was chatting with and encouraging the children in the area.

Transforming Employee Benefits

Henry built two large facilities with similar offerings. The Sarah Heinz House for poor children contained the same facilities he pioneered for his employees. These included a gymnasium, pool, recreation center, classrooms for training in skilled labor, library, bathing and changing rooms, and much more. The children's center had boarding rooms for homeless children. Female employees had uniforms to save their street clothes and a free manicure department. The manicure department served for their enjoyment and ensured their hands that touched food products were always as clean as possible. Henry was the first entrepreneur to offer such extravagant services to employees, all provided for free to all employees at Henry's expense. All of this was considered astounding by the business community. To provide such services to poor children was beyond comprehension for the citizens of his day. Yet Henry trusted God that company profits could indefinitely continue to fund these efforts.

In an age when workers received low pay and no benefits for long hours and sometimes dangerous working conditions, Henry single-handedly created the employee benefits concept.

He didn't stop there. Many manufacturers opposed the 1906 Pure Food and Drug Act. Henry earned their ire by becoming a strong proponent of the law. He also offered factory tours to the general public, which nobody else was doing. During these tours, he could demonstrate how the safety for workers and cleanliness benefited customers throughout his manufacturing process. Because of all this, people felt they could trust

Henry and the safety of his manufactured food products.

Not all his care for workers and the poor were so broad. He was also a master of the small gesture. One older female employee walked along part of Henry's same path to work. One day as they walked together, Henry remarked they were both getting older and should not exert themselves as much anymore in getting to work. From then on, until she retired, Henry sent a chauffeured car to pick her up each morning and return her home each evening, even though she was only a secretary. And Henry continued to walk to work.

Transforming the "Red Light" District

Henry also engaged in political efforts. For example, he tried to get local politicians and police to clean up the "red light" district since he pointed out that prostitution is un-biblical and disrespects women. When the politicians claimed such a cleanup effort would be hopeless, Henry quietly purchased properties within that area, starting his own real estate department. He eventually bought several hundred properties. He fixed these properties as needed and hired detectives to screen the background of tenants. All applicants who engaged in illegal or immoral activities which damaged the community were rejected. He gradually attracted small businesses and working-class people, generating many jobs and turning around that community into a safe, stable environment, all at no cost to the taxpayers.

In the process, he earned a 5 percent return on his rentals due to the increasing stable, higher quality tenants. Eventually, other landlords followed his example in avoiding bad tenants so they would not continue to lose money. He also paid employees from his personal funds to tour the best flood control districts of Europe. Henry then commissioned a report to apply those world-class standards to Pittsburgh's frequent flooding problems.[69] He eventually cajoled municipal, county, state, and federal officials into considering the plan he paid for. It took longer than his lifetime to convince recalcitrant government officials to implement the plan across several states. This personally funded effort eventually saved many lives and much property damage.

His report is the basis of flood control concepts in America today.

Lasting Impact

When he declared bankruptcy, he was thirty-one with a wife and two children (they eventually had four), which would have been devastating to many people. Yet Henry began again, trusting God would bless his efforts to bring fresh, high-quality food to a broader number of people at a more affordable price. God responded indeed—blessing Henry, his family, his company, the growing number of his charitable efforts around Pittsburgh, and the many people Henry sought to help. In the process, Henry had become prosperous within just ten years of his bankruptcy.

---

[69] Pittsburgh has three rivers flowing through the city.

By the time of Henry's death at age seventy-four, the little startup company had grown over its forty-three years after his bankruptcy to a point where it had 6,523 employees in twenty factories distributed throughout America, Canada, and Europe, harvesting over 100,000 crops from more than 100,000 acres under cultivation plus contracts with many farmers. The company owned 258 railroad freight cars to move products from its 55 regional warehouses and agencies in every leading commercial center throughout the world. His 952 salesmen were based on every inhabited continent.

As impressive as the enterprise he built sounds, Henry was not interested in money. Instead, he focused daily on maximizing efficiency from every day and every activity to help the most people. He lived by the saying, "We get out of life what we put into it."

Henry had an enormous and lasting impact on worker relations. His revolutionary ideas on treating workers are now considered standard practice to motivate and care for employees. His style of entrepreneurial leadership was Christlike servant leadership. His charitable thoughts carried a worldwide impact still reflected today. Henry's will began by stating his faith in Jesus was the inheritance he received, which sustained him in all his lifelong endeavors, and which he wished to pass onto others—not just his family—as his true legacy. In response to Henry's concern for people he met in his travels, the Japanese government and business leaders sent telegrams of condolences. 2,000 Japanese school children traveled to Pittsburgh to attend his funeral.

Like so many entrepreneurs, Henry did not see any separation between his business and family, nor between faith and business. Throughout his entire life, he never failed to attend a church service every Sunday, no matter where in the world he was. He lived his faith all seven days of the week, seeing his business as a marketplace-based ministry to help others rather than solely for his profit. As he pointed out to many people, Henry's Christian life helped him build a successful business reputation, and his business enabled him to make his Christian life effective in its practical service to others. He worked up to the very day he died of pneumonia—with travel tickets in his pocket to promote Christian training.

Perhaps most reflective of his Christian ministry in the workplace was the reaction of his employees to his death. His employees loved him so much they built a statue of him at their own expense in the Heinz headquarters in Pittsburgh. They wept exceedingly at his memorial service. For many years afterward, when managers suggested changes in employee processes, employees would refuse to change. They'd say, "Mr. Heinz himself told me to do it this way."

13

Consumer Desires, Atlanta, and Coca-Cola: Asa Candler

"...Sell all that you have and distribute to the poor,
and you will have treasure in heaven; and come, follow me."
— Luke 18:22

Asa Candler

1851-1929

In his famous letter to the Roman church, Paul wrote chapter 12 verse 2, "Do not be conformed to this world, but be transformed by the renewal of your mind..." Of course, this is much easier to say than to actually do for many people, including Christians, particularly when immersed in a monolithic cultural perspective that runs counter to some of God's Word. Asa Candler grew up in such a culture, but as both an entrepreneur and as a Christian, he could at least partially overcome cultural problems to improve society.

Asa's father, Samuel, inherited a Georgia plantation near the Alabama border, where he owned many slaves. Samuel was also a member of the Georgia state legislature. As such, he was heavily involved in politics, during the volatile 1850s and early 1860s and leading up to and throughout the Civil War. His brother Milton, who was fourteen years older than Asa, both served in the Confederate army and was elected to the Georgia House of Representatives during the war. Milton served several terms in the United States Congress and also served as a delegate to the Democratic National Convention several times after the Reconstruction Era.

Asa was the fourth youngest of eleven children. One of his younger brothers, Warren, was short of height[70] but high in intellect, graduating college in only two years and eventually becoming a Senior Bishop in the Methodist Church. Upon the crushing defeat of the Confederacy and the federal government freeing all the slaves, Samuel lost everything, and the family became impoverished.

This family context of slave ownership, economic catastrophe due to losing their slaves, and the prevalent attitudes of his generation contributed to an infected moral viewpoint which Asa never quite overcame. Asa was only nine when the war began, and just fourteen when it ended. The family tried to work the farm themselves during the chaotic post-war years when the Southern economy had collapsed. Asa, however, left home in 1870 at the age of nineteen to find employment as a drugstore clerk and manufacturer of patent medicines in the

---

[70] His students later called him "King Shorty."

big and newly rebuilt city of Atlanta—which had been burned by the Union General William T. Sherman Confederate Army in a retreat from the city near the end of the Civil War.

While working as a drugstore clerk, he met John Pemberton,[71] an ex-Confederate volunteer cavalry officer who had received a saber chest wound in the final month of the war. John had been a pharmacist before starting the war, so he used this knowledge to self-treat his pain. First, he experimented with alternatives to morphine, then extracts from the coca tree, from which cocaine is manufactured. Finally, John developed a liquid medicine that included both cocaine and alcohol. He marketed it as an elixir for "highly-strung Southern women and all those whose sedentary employment causes nervous prostration." However, to put it more bluntly, the compound was targeted at fellow ex-Confederate soldiers who could not find work in the devastated Southern post-war economy, and who thus suffered from drug addiction, depression, and alcoholism. These were also the symptoms—particularly drug and alcohol addiction—from which John was trying desperately to escape himself.

Asa's original intent upon leaving home was to become a doctor. However, he abandoned this idea within two years because it offered too little income in the post-war ravaged Southern economy. As a wholesale druggist, he lived in the back of the store. His dad died during this time in 1872. When his older brother contracted typhoid, Asa took over the family store in rural western Georgia. In 1875 he returned to Atlanta

---

[71] 1831-1888

and to the same pharmacy he had worked in previously. There, he also became an active church officer.

Seizing Opportunity

His first opportunity for self-employment arose when the drug store owner, Mr. Howard, relocated to another town: Asa and a partner opened their own drug store. Mr. Howard was not pleased. He posted ads that discouraged customers from buying at Asa's drugstore. Asa would not remain quiet. He aggressively responded with his own attack ads. His ads implied that he was the one maintaining product quality. Further, Asa traded on their location as the successor to the old Howard stand.

During Asa's initial entrepreneurial growth phase, the City of Atlanta and Fulton County enacted temperance legislation in 1886, forcing people such as John Pemberton to divest his product of all alcohol. John looked for substitutes, settling on the kola nut which contained caffeine. One day he accidentally blended the original syrup recipe with carbonated water. The resulting taste, which he and friends enjoyed, was named Coca-Cola. John decided to market this new result—no longer as medicine—but as a new fountain drink.

Soon after John began marketing Coca-Cola to the general public, he fell ill again and nearly went bankrupt. In desperation, he sold partial rights to his secret formula to several business partners. He hoped to generate enough money to subsidize his morphine addiction yet still retain an ownership share in the new formula that he could leave his only son. However, shortly after John died in 1888, his son sold the remaining rights to the formula for a reported five hundred dollars to Asa. The new owner promptly engaged in an aggressive marketing campaign, and sales began to blossom. Asa kept his personal expenditures very low, while the other two partners did not. By 1891, Asa had gradually purchased their entire interests as they came to owe him more money. Some reports suggest he may have acquired ownership interests for around a total of $2,500.

Transforming Sales Models

Initially, Asa did all the production work himself. He refined the formula based on customer desires and cooked batches of syrup on a crude vat. In 1899, two Chattanooga attorneys approached him. They presented a business plan: Allow franchise owners to be granted a license that would allow them to bottle the drink, and sell it to local franchises. Up to that time, Coca-Cola was only available as a fountain drink in Atlanta drugstores and some of the new ice cream parlor stores just coming into vogue. The soda fountain store would not become common following the invention of a carbon dioxide tank in 1888 until the early 1900s, when the tanks became cost-effective. The attorneys' idea of a franchise model suddenly opened up a massive market for Asa.

Applying the master franchise concept, generally unknown at that time, Asa could rapidly expand his business nationwide with no borrowing and minimal capital needed on his part.

In fact, the master franchises required almost no outlay by the company except for some advertising. Further sales of individual franchises by the master franchisees gave Asa more cash to expand production facilities and advertising exposure. Meanwhile, master franchisees did all the work of finding those additional franchisees.

At this same time in American history, publishers began to develop national magazines, opening up the new opportunity for Asa as an early adopter of this new venue to take out countrywide ads promoting his drink more economically than ever before. More cash flow combined with lower cost and greater marketing exposure, smartly boosted by aggressive marketing campaigns Asa personally developed and pushed in every publishing outlet he could find, built strong brand recognition rapidly. He preferred to reinvest nearly all profits into growing the company. Asa both pioneered the master franchise concept and largely invented the idea of national brand-building and advertising campaigns.

The only major obstacle inhibiting growth was the political movement of Progressivism. Today, a similar movement might be termed leftists, liberals, or big government advocates. As Progressive candidates gradually took over American political offices, they pressed for excessive profits taxes to force redistribution of profits from those who earned it to other politically favored groups. Worse, some tax provisions were specifically directed against the Coca-Cola company, its products, and Asa personally.

Asa insisted on a paternal relationship with all franchisees. He also prohibited every employee and franchisee from consuming alcohol. He sought an orderly society based on Biblical principles and was willing to work with anyone who supported these traditional values. Sadly, as noted earlier, he was still influenced by his cultural surroundings, stating he "did not see Negros as his equals, nor lesser whites were either." However, he provided jobs to Black Americans and poorer whites.

Transforming Atlanta

Asa applied his large fortune to improve society through both social and political actions. He consistently taught Sunday School from very early in his adult life. He donated abundantly—particularly to what is now Emory University. These donations built Emory into the most prestigious institution in Atlanta. His younger brother Warren—who by this time had graduated from Emory and become both a teacher and a bishop in the Methodist Church—became president of Emory. The brothers worked together to support and guide many Methodist institutions. For example, Asa endowed many chemistry department chairs, classrooms, a library, and a reading room. Asa also gave millions to what became Emory Hospital.

In 1908 he was active in the child labor law movement to protect children from dangerous factory work. Unlike other business owners of that time, Asa was willing to work with organized unions anywhere in the country. During this time, he opened a series of Candler Buildings, such as the one in

Atlanta,[72] Baltimore,[73] and New York,[74] all of which still stand as major landmarks in each city. He was also chairman of the Atlanta Chamber of Commerce, working hard to bring prosperity to the residents of Atlanta, which in some ways was still recovering from the massive war damage.

Atlanta prospered, but that prosperity was not shared equally. The city grew from a population of 89,000 in 1900 to more than 150,000 only ten years later—a more than two-thirds increase in a short period as people poured in from all over the country looking for jobs after the Panic of 1893, which was a depression lasting until 1897. The rapidly increasing competition for jobs, not keeping pace with actual job creation, caused inevitable growing labor tension. Adding to this was the general culture of Atlanta since its founding. The first three mayors were members of the Free and Rowdy Party, promoting saloons and prostitution as their idea of economic development. While some citizens objected, the Christians rarely had enough political clout to tamp down this legalization of vice in order to generate tax revenue.

However, it all came to a head on September 22, 1906, when the local paper ran an unsubstantiated accusation that black men had raped white women. This triggered a massive race riot where enraged and often drunken white mobs, spurred on by the Democratic mayor, murdered and maimed many African American citizens, in what could be viewed as a

---

[72] 1906. At that time, the tallest in the city.

[73] 1912

[74] 1914

precursor to the Tulsa Massacre of 1921. They destroyed black-owned businesses for two days until the governor called in the Georgia National Guard. Shamefully, some members of law enforcement may have cheered on the rioters before stopping the violence.

In response, Mayor Woodward, then in his second term, called for restrictions on the civil rights of blacks under a group of unjust laws commonly referred to as Jim Crow laws. However, the infamous Jim Crow laws in no way solved the problem. It would continue to simmer for years after the riot under three more mayors and through Woodward's third and final term.

It was in this political context that Asa was elected in 1917. Asa would follow Woodward's mayoral tenure as a two-year term mayor, ending his daily management of Coca-Cola Company. During his brief term, Asa sought biblical solutions to the tension in the city. He formed a committee of evangelists and business leaders, black and white, called the Commission on Interracial Cooperation. This group provided a channel for black city residents to participate in developing solutions to social ills. It opposed lynching, mob violence, and peonage (unfair work conditions). The Commission eventually evolved into today's Southern Regional Council, which advocated for racial equality during World War II.

As mayor, Asa pushed hard for strict enforcement of the city prohibition law against alcohol. He also strongly encouraged prostitutes to leave their lifestyle, simultaneously taking out advertisements educating the public on the significant negative impact prostitution was having on families, workers,

131

and the city. During his term as mayor, he used advertising campaigns in the same manner as he had in business: increasing the public's awareness of societal ills. Another moral innovation he promoted was mediation. A form of legal redress, mediation talks between employers and their employees was a substitute to the court system, which could impose punitive actions that neither party desired. Rather, mediation attempted to reconcile employer and employee in a non-hostile fashion.

As Atlanta's Mayor during World War I, Asa attempted to get the federal government to build a large army base in Atlanta. He was partially successful in attracting jobs to the city to relieve the imbalance between the quickly increasing number of residents and the more limited volume of jobs available. These attempts to improve the quality of life and better the societal situation had a lasting impact over the coming decades, leading to today's Atlanta culture, which is much more respectful of fellow residents. As in business, Asa made amazing gains in his civic efforts.

Unfortunately, personal hardship was thrust upon him once again. He had gone from a childhood of privilege to teen and early adult years of poverty, then gradually became a wealthy man. In 1919, his beloved wife Lucy died, giving him much grief and perhaps causing his unwillingness to run for a second term as mayor. In response, he withdrew from the public spotlight. During that same year, he gave most of his stock in Coca-Cola Company to his children, who later sold it to an investor group in 1922.[75]

In his grief, he had troubled relationships with two women which, rather than relieving, only compounded his grief: The first, a New Orleans socialite, encouraged him towards marriage and sued him when he broke off the engagement for breach of promise. The second woman was one of his secretaries. He married her, decided to divorce her, but then relented despite their broken relationship. He remained married to her until his death.

While he may have been unhappy in his personal life towards the end, he remained generous. Throughout the later period of his life, from 1919 till his stroke in 1926, he gave away nearly all of his fortune to charitable purposes: He benefited all city residents in various ways and funded sharing the Gospel of Jesus with people across the nation. While he could not entirely break free of the supremacist values of his early upbringing during a tumultuous time, he professed to do his duty as he best understood it without counting the personal cost. In particular, he kept in mind the warning of the parable of the rich young man who knew to point towards righteous behavior but stayed captive to his wealth and societal standing. Instead, Asa was determined to be a faithful steward of God's wealth. He gave away nearly everything in the spirit of the lesson he learned from this Biblical parable.

---

[75] This year he also donated more than 50 acres to the city to create Candler Park for all city residents to enjoy.

14

Overcoming Racial Prejudice and Adversity: Part I

"I have learned that success is to be measured
not so much by the position that one has reached in life
as by the obstacles which he has overcome
while trying to succeed."
— Booker T. Washington

Booker T. Washington

1856–1915

The American Civil War was arguably the result of the 1840s Second Great Awakening religious revival. The Second Great Awakening's recognition that God never condones treating any human beings as mere property was a dramatic, course-shifting event for the nation. It still affects American citizens today.

Earlier in this book, we looked at this era of seismically disruptive change from the viewpoint of Christian brothers—the Tappans—living in the north where slavery had been abolished peacefully. In the previous chapter, we saw the same period from the viewpoint of a Christian coming out of a slave-holding family and culture. Now, we will turn to look at how a Christian slave might transform society as an entrepreneur.

Booker was born a slave on a small plantation in southwestern Virginia. Although he was never told anything about when he was born, he estimated the year to be 1856. For the first nine years, he lived with his enslaved mother. He never knew who his father was. As he grew up, Booker recalled the slave master was so demanding that the family was never allowed to sit down together for dinner. Occasionally, they were tossed, "a piece of bread here and a scrap of meat there. It was a cup of milk at one time and some potatoes at another, very much as dumb animals get theirs."

Near the end of the Civil War, Union troops showed up at the farm. It was the Spring of 1865. As they approached the area, the singing from the slave quarters grew louder and bolder, with more enthusiasm than ever before, lasting late into the night. The next morning, a Union officer rode up and read Lincoln's famous Emancipation Proclamation—announcing freedom from slavery. All were now free to go wherever they wished when they pleased.

Booker's mother Jane took her family to West Virginia to join her husband, Washington Ferguson, who had escaped slavery during the war. Booker was illiterate before arriving in West Virginia—It was illegal for Virginia slaves to learn to read.

Once in West Virginia Virginia, Booker worked hard to teach himself reading, and he attended school for the first time.

A Transformative Education

It was there he encountered a new dilemma: The school he began attending required a last name—which slaves were never given. Like so many other former slaves, he would have to choose a new name. His mother had sometimes used the name Talliaferro.[76] Booker, however, chose his step-father's name—Washington—and also decided to use Talliaferro, which the family had immediately discarded upon liberation, as a middle name.

Booker worked in the coal mines for several years to earn money and help support the family. His initial exposure to education at the schoolhouse in West Virginia ignited a passion for learning as much as possible. Upon discovering Union General Samuel C. Armstrong's Hampton Academy for new freedmen, he began to dream of what could be. Booker saved to make the 400-mile journey to enroll at this rare opportunity for a young black man. The study program required four years of eight to ten-hour classroom days plus a minimum of two hours in the evening except for Sundays—an amazing opportunity to expand his learning.

During the Reconstruction period,[77] Booker worked in the coal

---

[76] Perhaps the name of the man who impregnated her.

[77] 1867–1878

mines from age eleven—then as a janitor at Hampton Institute to earn his tuition. He graduated in 1875 with high honors. Following graduation, he moved to Malden, West Virginia, where he witnessed a large battle between freedmen and the Klu Klux Klan terrorist group.

Within a couple of years, he had the opportunity to teach in Washington, DC for one year while attending Wayland Seminary. Booker noted the contrast between those in Washington who could afford some comfort versus the very poor at Hampton who had to work for everything. This caused him to return to Hampton to teach the first class of 120 Native Americans in 1879 who had been prisoners of war from Florida tribes and whom the federal government was attempting to "civilize."

As former Confederate officers and politicians overthrew elected governments in the South,[78] and Northerners became weary of the constant military cost of protecting blacks and Republican whites, the Reconstruction period came to an end. The change was signaled, in part, by the withdrawal of federal troops who had enforced the rule of law and protection of citizens throughout the South after the Civil War. Hostile ex-Confederates organized politically in the Democratic Party and militarily as the Klu Klux Klan, enacted laws to restrict black citizens' rights. These laws are collectively referred to as Jim

---

[78] Frequently through violence, threats, and intimidation.

Crow laws.[79] In this harsh environment, racial prejudice raged. This bigotry included not only many Southern whites but also Native Americans.

This time in his life taught Booker patience and strengthened his ability to maintain calm, continuing to advance his goals in the face of irrational hate and condescension. Miss Mary F. Mackie, one of his Hampton teachers, had taught him the importance of cleanliness, of educated people's willingness to perform menial labor, and of keeping oneself clean and orderly at all times. These lessons helped Booker build and maintain his character for a lifetime. A ten-hour school day, six days per week, created a strong work ethic, discipline, and solidified Booker's desire and ability to achieve his goals. And he would have many goals.

Transforming Education for His People

At age twenty-five, in 1881, General Armstrong sent him to become the first leader of a new school called Tuskegee Normal and Industrial Institute for Colored Teachers. The American Missionary Association was prepared to sponsor the new school, as they had for his alma mater, Hampton Institute. Tuskegee had an unusual founding that reflected Booker's life work: It was founded by a former slave and a former slaveholder, who both promoted the idea of a school

---

[79] It would be decades before the damage these laws caused to the rights of African-Americans began to be undone: Jim Crow laws were overruled by the Civil Rights Act of 1964 and the Voting Rights Act of 1965, though culturally their impact lasts until the present day.

to educate black people in Alabama.

In context, 25 percent of white children over age ten were illiterate, with very few graduating from high school, and government-supported schools open to black children were extremely rare. Approximately 25 percent of whites and 38 percent of blacks entering first grade at government-run schools left in their first month, unable to pay the required tuition. In other words, public education was grossly inadequate in that era, and the state legislature was not inclined to provide sufficient funding, so the possibility of obtaining money for a black school seemed remote.

During this bigoted period, blacks were still the majority of voters in Macon County, Alabama, before Jim Crow laws made it impossible for most of them to vote within a few years. The Democratic candidate, a former Confederate colonel made a deal with the Republican black candidate (the ex-slave who wanted to start a school) that if blacks would vote for the Democrat in the 1880 election instead of their usual Republican candidate, the Democrat would use his connections in the state legislature to obtain funding for a new school for blacks. The black Republicans honored the deal, and the Democrat also kept his word by arranging for a one-time $2,000 appropriation for salaries only, not land, building, or classroom supplies. The racially mixed board then contacted General Armstrong, imploring him to send someone to launch and run the school. This is the state of affairs Booker entered into.

Booker showed incredible entrepreneurial ingenuity. He began classes in a rundown abandoned church and shanty, immediately promoting private fund-raising efforts. Within a year, he was able to purchase a former one hundred acre plantation for 500 dollars. He set students to work building classrooms and dormitories, plus constructing all the furniture as part of their work-study program to learn building trades. He also encouraged local citizens to rebuild the short Tuskegee Railroad spur line (only 5-1/2 miles long) damaged during the Civil War. This, in turn, connected to other railroad networks, which eventually allowed local businesses to connect the rural little town and the new school to the bigger city of Selma eighty-five miles away, re-opening commercial opportunities for all residents and students.

Based on his Hampton Institute experiences, Booker set out to train students in skills, morals, and religious life in addition to academic subjects and practical trades. He urged graduates to return to former plantation areas and show people feeling hopeless in rural areas how to inject new energy and ideas into farming and deepen their moral, intellectual and religious life. He also emphasized self-reliance.

In just a couple of years, Booker borrowed $250 from the Hampton treasurer's personal funds to invest that money in a lifelong quest to seek donations from people throughout America and eventually Europe. The donations he received were carefully and frugally spent. For example, the first major campus building cost $6,000 in building materials due to free student labor and teacher supervision, versus an estimated contractor cost of $20,000 or more. Donations for this first building and future ones came in small amounts of cash, animals, crops, and various materials. This included one local white sawmill owner who insisted on supplying all the lumber secured only by Booker's personal promise to eventually pay when he could raise the money. This first building, Porter Hall, was erected and maintained through many cash crises with donations of the exact amount needed arriving just in time, sent providentially by people indicating they were motivated from God's prodding.

Booker rapidly added teachers, students, facilities, and new programs. He taught teachers who started their own schools throughout the South, promoting Booker's ideas of practical and intellectual education combined with religious training and an emphasis upon becoming self-reliant. He taught the practical skills needed for students, who came predominantly from rural Southern communities, to succeed at farming and other trades. Booker emphasized that all labor is practical, beautiful, and dignified, as God intended it to be. While teaching this, he kept tuition for needy students to nearly nothing. Students earned all or part of their tuition and living expenses by learning and engaging in construction projects, agriculture, and domestic work associated with the campus. Students also raised crops and livestock on campus grounds and manufactured some goods such as furniture.

By 1890, white Democrats had firmly entrenched racial seg-regation in the South. Jim Crow laws began to disenfranchise and suppress, and would successfully disenfranchise black people throughout the South for the next seven decades. Yet, Booker was able to build a teaching staff to provide industrial education, particularly utilizing air, water, steam, electricity, horsepower, and anything else he could think of to improve the productivity of students and graduates. His focus on improving productivity was relentless, even in the face of Jim Crow.

Booker's desire to better help his people did not go unopposed. White farmers began to complain that Booker's students were too educated and were too lazy to do manual labor. This would cause local agricultural productivity to suffer and lead to public support burdens, they argued. Booker fought back. He personally studied how to make bricks, constructed a brick-making factory on the campus, and showed local whites that black education would not cost them anything, but instead substantially boosted local prosperity for everyone.

The story does not end here, though. Booker still has many goals left to accomplish. In our next chapter, we will dive into the intellectual legacy of Booker, his conflict with Southern society and its militant opposition to Black prosperity, and Booker's infamous rivalry with DuBois.

15

Overcoming Racial Prejudice and Adversity: Part I

"He lifted the veil of ignorance from his people and pointed the way to progress through education and industry."
— Lifting the Veil Monument

Booker T. Washington

1856-1915

In an 1895 speech, Booker initiated his Atlanta Compromise. This compact was between him as Tuskegee Institute President, other black leaders, and Southern white leaders. It said that Southern blacks would work with white Democrat political rule. These white leaders would, in turn, guarantee basic education and respect for due process civil rights for blacks. Blacks would not agitate for equality or integration. They would even tolerate voting disenfranchisement. And white Northern Republicans would fund black educational charities in the South.

Booker's vision was one of gradual, hard-won social change. He did not intend for the Atlanta compromise to last forever. Rather, his plan was to send his educated graduate corp into the rural South to earn the respect of Southern whites as productive citizens, rather than demanding political influence immediately from a still humiliated, angry, defeated ex-Confederate—now Democrat—leadership. He hoped to win full equality through example and by building black economic prosperity without the risk of violence and harm. In the face of Southern white hostility, most Southern blacks agreed with Booker. However, there was one major exception to this rule—William Edward Burghardt Du Bois.

Intellectual Battles

Booker and W.E.B. DuBois[80] values were fundamentally opposed. They eventually clashed when DuBois openly gathered other black leaders in Niagara, New York, in 1905 to make a public declaration demanding political action immediately.

DuBois grew up in tolerant Massachusetts and completed graduate degrees from the University of Berlin and Harvard.[81] He earned his undergraduate degree from Fisk University in Nashville, Tennessee.[82] DuBois eventually accepted a professorship of history, sociology, and economics at the all-black Atlanta University in 1897, just a few years before the

---

[80] 1868-1963

[81] He was the first black American to earn a doctorate there.

[82] It was there he first was exposed to Southern white racism.

Atlanta race riot of 1906. In 1909, DuBois was one of the founders of the National Association for the Advancement of Colored People (NAACP) and moved to New York to work for the new civil rights organization. There he joined the Socialist Party of America, but supported Democrat President Woodrow Wilson, who drove black employees out of the federal government.

DuBois was something of a political pragmatist. After World War II, for example, DuBois supported communism worldwide. DuBois had finally begun to sway other blacks to shift away from Booker's approach for earning full equality (politically, socially, etc.) by first building economic prosperity and self-sufficiency. DuBois's position demanded instant equality through political agitation and professional jobs rather than Booker's training for mostly industrial trades. What most people did not know—until after Booker's death—was his frequent secret funding of lawsuits challenging Jim Crow laws and other violations of Black citizens' rights, which he was able to pay for from profits generated from his many business startups under the Tuskegee Institute umbrella.

DuBois became famous for his efforts, both in the U.S. and abroad. The first president of the new nation of Ghana invited DuBois to visit, which he eventually did in 1960. The following year, Ghana appropriated funds for DuBois's idea of an African diaspora encyclopedia. At age ninety-three, DuBois moved to Ghana, where he died two years later.

The tension between these two solutions would not be resolved until Dr. Martin Luther King Jr. led the great non-violent civil rights movement in the 1960s—almost half a century after Booker's death.

Orator & Educator

Booker lectured alongside great orators in Carnegie Hall, including Mark Twain, Joseph Choate, and Robert Ogden, in a campaign that raised 1.8 million dollars for Tuskegee. Henry Rogers and Booker first met when Booker spoke to a large crowd in Madison Square Garden in New York. Rogers was so impressed that he funded sixty-five black schools during the next fifteen years until his death and provided large contributions to Tuskegee and Hampton institutes. Rogers and Booker became close personal friends. When Rogers died suddenly after a heart attack, the Rogers family arranged for Booker to ride the length of Rogers's Virginian Railway in Rogers's personal private railroad car. Both black and white citizens warmly received Booker at each stop, where he made speeches.

Speaking engagements arrived from groups of Northern white Republicans, who became his main donor base. Private chats with wealthy benefactors included John Rockefeller, Andrew Carnegie, and many other wealthy people. Andrew Carnegie paid $20,000 to build a library for the school at the time Booker started a night school in 1884 for students who had full-time jobs during the day.

Through these discussions, Booker developed his understanding that wealthy people desired to use their fortunes to accomplish things, including philanthropy for the poor, but taxing and vilifying them would result in less charitable support for society and far fewer jobs. Booker appreciated the influence of the rich: He could use their donations and support for his cause. Eventually—Booker must have allowed himself to dream—the education he fought for would help address economic equality, and in turn would allow members of his own community to join the ranks of the wealthiest individuals in America.

In the meantime, Booker's strategy seemed to have worked. Many rich people, especially in Boston, thanked Booker for the privilege of being allowed to contribute funds towards helping others. He also realized they wanted accountability for generous donations and preferred to leverage their charity. Tuskegee's programs accomplished that for both students and donors alike.

Booker also gave speeches to Northern audiences, where he solicited donations, but he never charged a speaker fee and never asked for any personal remuneration. Black audiences were exhorted with the importance of industrial and technical education in addition to academic and religious training to help them become self-sufficient and escape the sharecropper situation that replaced the old slave plantation system in the South. Booker encouraged Southern white audiences to work with blacks to rebuild the South to bring prosperity to both races and work towards racial harmony.

Booker cleverly learned to address each type of audience in a way that furthered the goal of improving race relations. His biggest challenge was a request from the black and white citizens of Atlanta to accompany them to Washington. There, he testified as their key witness and champion before Congress for an appropriation towards funding the Atlanta Exposition The exposition intended to highlight the progress both races had made since the end of the Civil War thirty years earlier. Booker successfully convinced Congress to make the grant. The leadership in Atlanta then asked him to speak at the opening ceremony for the Exposition. This was a major challenge too.

How could he craft a message to a very mixed audience of Northerners, Southern white elites who were formerly slaveholders, and blacks in a way that might be acceptable to everyone and which might benefit all of them? The three groups were still very opposed to each other. To add to the pressure, Booker was first courteously treated in a large parade. The Georgia governor enthusiastically shook his hand, heralding Booker as a genius on race relation solutions.

Booker's speech featured an analogy of a hand working together for the common benefit, yet with the five fingers separate as to the issue of social acceptance. Grover Cleveland, the only Democrat president to speak with Booker, visited the Negro building at the Exposition, which featured exhibits from Tuskegee and Hampton. After reviewing their exhibits, the President noted that wealthy and powerful people who are the happiest are those who do the most for others. He also recognized that racial prejudice among both races holds back the ignorant bigot, not the person the bigot is hostile towards, as Booker had proved.

Booker organized an annual Negro Conference in 1890 to bring between 800 to 900 black leaders to Tuskegee for discussing how to improve the industrial, mental, and moral conditions of the Black race. He also founded the Negro Business Association. He was a deeply committed Christian who insisted on high-quality Christian education and believed rural blacks in the South needed good Christian education to succeed.

To that end, he wrote a letter commenting on the dismal state of black teachers and ministers in many rural black churches. This caused the ministers to condemn him. Eventually, bishops looked into his charges, pressured by the public, and found that Booker was correct to point out this injustice. In response, the situation began to change rapidly. Helped by training from Tuskegee, which had always emphasized a Christian education, but was—and still is—non-denominational, change was coming.

A Lifetime of Achievements

Booker proved to be very astute at politics and networking.

He became good friends with Julius Rosenwald,[83] part-owner, and an officer of Sears, Roebuck & Company. Rosenwald joined Tuskegee's board and gave millions to the school, as well as many other black educational institutions throughout the South. Rosenwald also created a fund requiring local communities to raise matching funds to construct and operate

---

[83] 1862-1932

more than 5,000 schools in small Southern communities. This encouraged collaboration between blacks and whites.

Tuskegee architects developed the model plans, some students helped build the schools, and its teacher graduates staffed many of the schools. Other benefactors who became his friends included Henry Rogers, President of Standard Oil, and George Eastman, founder of Eastman Kodak Company and developer of most of the photography industry.

By this time, Booker had earned international recognition for his entrepreneurial achievements. In building Tuskegee, and for leveraging the school's education and financial self-sufficiency to improve all aspects of life for all Southerners, helping to build a black middle class, Booker had created a legacy that would last into the 21st century.

In 1899, several prominent Bostonians paid for Booker and his third wife to have a restful vacation in Europe. Booker's biggest personal "flaw" was his lifelong tendency to drive himself with very long work hours—a habit that eventually led to his early death at age fifty-nine. His first and second wives, Fannie[84] and Olivia,[85] as well as his final wife, Margaret, who outlived him, all assisted him at Tuskegee. He pushed himself and sometimes his wives very hard.

One example stands out from 1893. He was offered opportunities to address the National Education Association and another

---

[84] Died in 1884.

[85] Died in 1889.

large group of Northern supporters in Boston and the Christian Workers Association in Atlanta. Despite his busy schedule, he took trains from Boston to Atlanta, arriving only thirty minutes before his speech—which was limited by organizers to only five minutes. He then boarded another train returning to Boston within sixty minutes! He said the entire couple of days were an answer to prayer and was received very well in the press in each city.

During his working European tour, he met with Mark Twain, Queen Victoria, and the elite in France, Belgium, and France. Attendees at these high society meetings included two United States Supreme Court justices who had opposed black equality, Fuller and Harlan, illustrating how Booker was changing attitudes through Christian patience and entrepreneurial success. American ambassadors in the United Kingdom and France hosted banquets in his honor.

Fresh off the heels of his European tour, the Governor of West Virginia invited him to Charleston, West Virginia. There, he was honored by top state dignitaries for his role in helping determine the location of the capital of West Virginia and for his many other civic contributions to that state. Booker had a large role in convincing the legislature to start and locate the new West Virginia State University in the poor Kanawha Valley where he had been a coal miner. Similar invitations and honors would rapidly follow in Atlanta and New Orleans.

General Armstrong, his old Hampton principal and mentor, visited Tuskegee towards the end of the general's life. All citizens of both races honored the general, who had fought

Southern whites during the Civil War, yet showed by example to Booker how to display Christian charity and concern for Southerners of both races after the war. The next year, in 1900, Booker again returned to Europe to supervise an exhibition of black industrial arts and achievements at a Paris fair.

The arts and sciences were always on Booker's mind. And he was willing to take a risk on new hires to advance these fields of study. It was Booker who hired George Washington Carver[86] as a professor and head of the Tuskegee Institute Agriculture Department in 1896. Carver—a botanist, environmentalist, and inventor—is best known for inventing more than one hundred applications for peanuts as a substitute for cotton to rejuvenate the worn-out soil. Carver's mobile classroom made him very popular among both black and white farmers throughout the South. Booker's work with Carver's discoveries created most of the American peanut industry and exemplified the general's teachings on Christian charity for all.

Booker's list of acquaintances and political connections did not stop there, however. Over the course of his lifetime, Booker knew four Republican presidents personally—McKinley, Harrison, Taft, and Roosevelt—all of whom supported Tuskegee and asked his advice on race relations. Teddy Roosevelt invited Booker to dine with him and his family at the White House. Harvard and Dartmouth granted honorary doctorates to him. In 1897, Booker visited Washington to personally ask President McKinley to visit Tuskegee. In response, the President and almost all of his cabinet came on December 16, 1897. The entire

---

[86] 1860s-1943

town was decorated to welcome the President. The Alabama legislature adjourned to visit Tuskegee, as did the governor, plus prominent generals from the Spanish-American War.

By this time, Booker had grown Tuskegee from a startup institution, with no money, a leaking shanty hen-house and abandoned church building, and thirty students with only himself as a teacher into a 2,300-acre campus[87] with forty buildings,[88] twenty-eight industrial departments, plus academic and religious departments with a staff of eighty-six instructors and even more executive and support staff members. The property, then valued at more than $300,000, was entirely debt-free, plus an endowment of $215,000—increased shortly after that to 1.5 million dollars. The student population of over 1,100 came from twenty-seven states and territories plus Africa, Cuba, Puerto Rico, Jamaica, and other foreign nations. The school was developing plans to expand educational offerings to Africa.

Somehow, with his busy duties leading Tuskegee, managing national and international speaking engagements, advising presidents, starting other schools, running expositions, and engaging in countless entrepreneurial and educational efforts, Booker managed to publish five books of his own.

He died as he lived—a busy entrepreneur. Collapsing from hypertension and overwork during a speaking tour in New

---

[87] With 700 acres cultivated by students growing all the school's food for students and for sale.

[88] All except four built by the students.

York, he rushed home to Tuskegee—and passed away a few hours later. He never had ceased to dream of what could be overcome.

During his lifetime, the United States had been through a Civil War, the Spanish-American War, numerous Indian wars, and he died a year after the commencement of World War I in addition to the domestic Reconstruction period and ex-Confederate backlash of the segregation period in the South, which held back the newly freed slaves. In this tumultuous environment, it is Booker's overcoming of all naysayers, opposition, and systemic oppression that stands out.

Booker was highly revered after his death. Buried near the Tuskegee University chapel, large crowds attended his funeral. He received many honors following his death, including becoming the first black American featured on a postage stamp and on a coin. He was the first black person to have an oceangoing vessel named in his honor. Several sites from his life have been designated as national, historical monuments, and numerous schools around the nation are named after him. Scott Joplin dramatized his White House dinner with President Roosevelt in an opera. Books and a film feature a fictional version of his life. At the center of the Tuskegee campus, the Booker T. Washington Monument, called Lifting the Veil, was dedicated in 1922 with the following inscription:

> *He lifted the veil of ignorance from his people and pointed the way to progress through education and industry.*

At the time of his death, he had built a student body of fifteen hundred and a school endowment of two million dollars. Most importantly, he built a strong Christian institution that still educates and influences American society today.

Perhaps the best illustration of how much he accomplished during a difficult era is reflected in a 1900 invitation from the Virginia Governor. The Governor himself, along with every member of the state legislature, city council, and citizens of both races in his native Virginia, honored him in Richmond, the former Confederate capital, in the state where he began life as a slave.

Booker T. Washington—a former slave who rose to world prominence—is highly praised as the foremost spokesman for his race and a celebrated American educator. He almost single-handedly fostered the black middle class and hardworking black entrepreneurs while improving family life through Christian education. For himself, Booker said:

> *I have learned that success is to be measured not so much by the position that one has reached in life as by the obstacles which he has had to overcome while trying to succeed.*

There is so much to respect, learn from, and admire about Booker's life and legacy. May we all have the same grace in the face of opposition as Booker, and the courage to believe that we can overcome.

16

Building Support for Growth and a Bachelor of Motorcycles

"God needs businessmen too."
— *Robert LeTourneu's Pastor*

Robert LeTourneu

1888-1969

Sometimes God enables an entrepreneur to move both men and mountains to achieve biblical benefits for other people. This was literally the case for Bob LeTourneau. Robert Le-Tourneau—known as Bob—was the grandson of a Huguenot French Canadian preacher he never really knew. Bob's parents and uncle moved across the United States, searching for jobs, even living briefly in Mexico. They were poor, just like Bob's grandparents had been. His mother insisted Bob attend church regularly. His dad was very strict and demanding of him and his brothers as workers.

Bob was not particularly good at school, but math suddenly made sense to him in fifth grade, so the schoolmaster passed him over sixth grade directly into seventh grade, which proved more than Bob could handle. Fellow seventh-graders repeatedly called him dumb, which caused him to drop out. Unsurprisingly, Bob remained primarily self-educated his entire life.

Bob had many odd jobs upon dropping out, such as cutting wood. He built his first plow at age twelve. The family moved from his native Vermont to Duluth, Minnesota, at the age of fourteen. During his time in Duluth learning the iron foundry trade, he studied a mechanics correspondence course but never completed any assignments before moving to Portland, Oregon.

In Portland, Bob worked for a Mr. Hill, who owned the East Portland Iron Works until it burned down, forcing Bob to move once again. Mr. Hill was a Christian, setting an excellent example for Bob. However, Mr. Hill was also very demanding, and the environment included many cursing construction workers. One very irritable German taught Bob how to weld and build his own engine on his own time after working very long days. Bob was scalded multiple times during this employment from the hot molten iron.

A revival session in Portland caused him to give his life to Jesus. Bob constantly tinkered with machines to improve their efficiency, even when more experienced men kept mocking his crazy ideas. When a cable snapped on one of his stump-clearing machines, he lost all of his front teeth due to his tinkering. His time in Portland helped him train in the "school of hard knocks"—both in industrial skills and in his faith walk.

The next move to San Francisco was at the invitation of a family friend to work in an ironworks factory as an apprentice. Before he could achieve any success, the San Francisco earthquake and fire of 1906 devastated the city, simultaneously making jobs extremely difficult to find or keep. Forced to move, he later obtained a welding job at Yerba Buena Power Plant and became familiar with electricity. In between times, he was a woodcutter in Portland for his brother, bricklayer, farmhand, gold miner for his dad and uncle who followed him to San Francisco, carpenter's laborer, ditch digger, and held other jobs in similar low-skill trades. These low-level job experiences proved valuable to him later in his career.

Bachelor of Motorcycles

In 1909 Bob took an auto correspondence course. After that, he declared himself a "Bachelor of Motorcycles" for the new auto industry and became a vehicle mechanic by taking apart and reassembling the motorcycle he purchased with the chopped wood he sold. Later that year, Bob first saw a scraper in action when working as a laborer on the Stanislaus River Bridge. In 1911 he put up $1,000 of his wood savings as his half of a new partnership to start Superior Garage in Stockton, California. He designed and constructed possibly the first building in California made solely for such auto repair work. His partner was responsible for sales while Bob did all the mechanical repair work. They made a modest profit, enough to obtain a dealership.

But it wasn't all just business during this time. In Stockton, in 1917, he fell in love with Evelyn. Her dad thought Bob would not amount to much, so he withheld his permission for them to marry. Since she was seventeen—underage to marry in California without parental consent—the couple ran away to Tijuana, Mexico to get married. Her father was so mad about this that he did not speak to Bob for seven years. However, the situation bordered on the ridiculous: During those seven years Bob still performed all the mechanical and machine repairs for his father-in-law's draying business.[89]

The same year they were married, Bob entered one of the cars he had bought and souped-up for a race. Unfortunately, the driver had a horrible accident and hit Bob. Bob broke his neck, which prevented his plan of earning a better income by entering the Army during World War I. Instead, he talked his way into getting a job at the Navy yard in Vallejo, where he learned electrical machinist and welding skills.

Returning to Stockton after the war, Bob found his business partner had run up a substantial debt buying liquor in anticipation of Prohibition. To conceal the purchases, he had refused to keep account books updated. Effectively, the bank and debtors could not tell what was owed and how much collateral was available. In response, Bob taught himself bookkeeping to balance the books while, at the same time, he repaired all

---

[89] A draught horse wagon hauling large commodities, agricultural products, goods, and sometimes other things.

the used cars his partner had taken in trade but failed to do anything with during the war.

Gradually, things went from bad to worse. Their dealership was with Saxon Motor Car Company—a car manufacturer that was initially the seventh-largest car manufacturer in the nation but which went bankrupt a few years after the end of World War I. So far, Bob was not making any progress towards building a stable, let alone prosperous, future. But he was very determined.

Gradually, he sold all the used cars. Unfortunately, he also discovered more debt generated by his business partner as he got the books balanced. In an attempt to become more financially stable, he made a deal with creditors to give away his half of the business to his partner, and gradually pay off a $5,000 note in exchange for being released from any future debt his ex-business partner might generate.

During this period, Bob repaired Hold Manufacturing Company crawler-tractors. Hold Manufacturing Company would eventually become Caterpillar. He worked at this job for $7 per day, clearing and leveling fields for ranchers contracting with Holt to use the company's tractor and towed scraper.

Transforming Machinery

On the side, Bob purchased a vacant lot from which to repair machines. He built several scrapers to address problems he experienced when clearing and leveling land. By 1929 his scraper building business seemed to show promise, so he incorporated R.G. LeTourneau, Inc. and very quickly accumulated $100,000 of debt designing and building large earth-moving machines.

This was revolutionary: At the time, no one had created such large machinery for this purpose. Not surprisingly, investors were hesitant to fund such a venture. Desperate for cash flow, Bob managed to win a subcontract from the construction genius entrepreneur Henry Kaiser[90] to build the Boulder Highway leading to the new Hoover Dam project from 1931-1936. While Bob lost money on this road construction project, he gained a personal relationship with Mr. Kaiser, who purchased all of Bob's inventions and his shop in hopes of making Bob work for him.

Instead, Bob insisted on staying independent and contracting with the Kaiser company and other construction firms. The second world war proved an enormous benefit to both men. Henry Kaiser became the greatest industrialist of the 1930s and 1940s, and he brought Bob and his company along with him on many construction projects. R. G. LeTourneau, Inc. rapidly became the largest earthmoving equipment manufacturer in the world. Even better, it became a military contractor—famously constructing machines for the army during World War II, especially designing them for the Navy Sea Bees and the Army Corp of Engineers.

Bob built two small factories in Stockton, retiring from construction to concentrate solely on manufacturing. To accom-

---

[90] 1882-1967

plish this, he opened a plant in Peoria, Illinois.[91] While the factory was being built, Bob manufactured his machines outdoors, until the building could be enclosed in 1935. He then expanded into Toccoa, Georgia,[92] helping R.A. Forrest—an evangelist and founder of Tocca Falls Bible College—create jobs and education for poor young men in northeastern Georgia.

In Toccoa, Bob pivoted to building machines that could conquer mountainous terrain. Rapid company growth due to high war demand for machines led to opening more plants in Rydalmere, New South Wales, Australia[93] and Vicksburg, Mississippi,[94] then finally Longview, Texas.[95]

In 1953, post-World War II, Bob sold all equipment manufacturing rights and three of the plants to Westinghouse Air Brake Company and retired. However, he retained the Vicksburg and Toccoa plants and added a Longview plant when the army offered an abandoned hospital for sale. In 1958, at age seventy, when the non-compete agreement he signed upon the sale of his company to Westinghouse Air Brake Company expired, he launched another earthmover manufacturing line. This time, he included transportation and material handling machines. The Pentagon awarded him special recognition for his efforts.

---

[91] He did so to follow the business The Holt Manufacturing Company generated for the business.

[92] 1938

[93] 1941

[94] 1942

[95] 1945

The Dean of Earthmoving

Bob continued to create so many more innovations that he became known as the Dean of Earthmoving. He also applied his God-given innovative talent to developing an electric wheel hub motor, among other projects. One leader in the heavy construction industry, George Atkinson, President of the Guy F. Atkinson Company, said, "There is hardly any place in the vast industry that has not benefited through the products of Mr. LeTourneau's inventive genius."

His innovations were decades ahead of his time. He used huge rubber tires instead of metal, developed flexible body movement to address difficult and unstable terrain, and created mobile offshore drilling rigs. Bob's hundreds of patents included low-pressure tires, two-wheel tractor units, electric wheel drive, and many more patents covering not only large earthmovers but also specialized tools and overhead cranes to make manufacturing processes cheaper and faster.

This last set of innovations gave him the ability to implement an increasing number of improvements at an ever-faster pace, snowballing the rate of innovation. His innovations and business model were so successful that the factories he established have supplied over 70 percent of all Allied earthmoving equipment worldwide from World War II onward. And this doesn't even scratch the surface of the civilian applications of his machinery beyond that.

Amusingly, the correspondence school he never finished sent him an engineering diploma fifty years after he started the course. This caused Bob, then age seventy-six, to remark, "So now I've got a diploma. Now I'm educated." The next year, he turned over the presidency and daily management of the company he had created to his son.

Despite his success as a businessman, he fundamentally remained an engineer, focused on product success. Throughout his career, he was always more comfortable working beside his engineers and factory workers than in an office. Until his second retirement in 1966, he was the Chief Engineer and designer for his companies.

"God's Money"

But Bob's corporate success is far from his only significant achievement. He held leadership positions in the Christian & Missionary Alliance Church and was president of both the Christian Business Men's Committee and the famous Gideons International, most noted for placing Bibles in hotel rooms.[96] For thirty years, he flew around the United States and abroad in his corporate airplane for Christian speaking engagements every week to further evangelism and discipleship of many people.

He applied Christian concepts in his business, which he viewed as a partnership with God. Back in 1919, Bob had sought the advice of his pastor regarding whether he should become

---

[96] An international evangelical mission organization to business people formed in 1930.

a missionary. His pastor shocked him with the advice that guided him for the rest of his life: "God needs businessmen too." From that point on, he saw his companies as platforms for marketplace ministry. He was an early adopter of corporate chaplaincy services for his employees during the 1930s in Peoria, which was where he first began to speak to business groups about Jesus.

For most of his early life, he tithed. In 1932 he made $32,000 but failed to tithe that year. The following year he lost nearly the same amount and was $100,000 in debt. After that, Bob determined to tithe every year afterward, and his profits soared during the Great Depression to several million dollars annually. Pondering that fortune, he further decided to set aside 90 percent of his salary and company profits for God, living on only 10 percent for the rest of his life. As Bob remarked to business associates, "It's not how much of my money I give to God, but how much of God's money I keep for myself."

Perhaps because of his lack of formal education, Bob promoted education for others. He had purchased an unused Longview, Texas military hospital and related land and buildings from the Army in 1946, which he later used in his second manufacturing business. In 1961 he converted this property again, this time into the LeTourneau Technical Institute—now known as LeTourneau University. His mission was to create an institution that would provide technical, mechanical, engineering, and traditional college courses in a Christian setting. His goal largely succeeded, and he achieved the goal of training missionary-technicians.

Bob's evangelism efforts expanded to a worldwide effort. In 1953, he launched a development project in Liberia with the unusual combination of goals for colonization for Liberian natives in an uninhabited area, land development, agricultural farms and plantations, livestock introduction, evangelism, and other charitable activities. Overall, the idea was to show a poor but growing economy how to expand prosperity in rural areas, become self-sufficient, and share the Gospel among the remote non-Christian minority. The next year, Bob established the same type of comprehensive project in Peru, whose economy was thriving but under the rule of a military dictator at that time. Approximately 19 percent of the population fell beneath the global poverty line at the time.

His charitable efforts did not stop there. In 1959, after giving over $10 million in direct aid for religious and educational efforts, he formed the LeTourneau Foundation with an additional $40 million. His foundation continued supporting many mission and educational projects long after his death. LeTourneau's legacy lives on, in both the individuals who have attended LeTourneau University and those who have benefited from the foundation he created—inspiring future generations of Christian entrepreneurs.

17

Creative Problem Solving and Mr. Tropicana

"...each tree is known by its own fruit....
The good person out of the good treasure of his heart produces
good..."
— Luke 6:43-45

Anthony Rossi

1900-1993

Not all Christian entrepreneurs engage in major societal change efforts. Some simply refresh others and quietly share the Gospel joy they experience, in the process causing significant spiritual and physical help to millions. Our next story is about this type of person.

A Trouble Maker, Earthquake, and War

Anthony, also known as Tony, was born to a middle-class family on the island of Sicily, part of the Kingdom of Italy. However, it was not long before he experienced difficult family situations. In 1908, when Tony was eight years old, his father suffered a major financial setback, from which the family would never recover. During that same year, his hometown of Messina experienced a massive earthquake,[97] which decimated the city.

Tony came from a big family of four brothers and two sisters. His mother died in childbirth when Tony was fourteen. When his uncle from America visited shortly after his mother's death, Tony became excited about the seemingly endless opportunities his uncle described. It seemed America offered an escape from the dismal life in Sicily.

Tony grew up as a Catholic, the state religion of Italy at the time, but he did not give much thought to the teachings of the Catholic Church. Until the earthquake, Tony had been known as somewhat of a troublemaker. However, the traumatic earthquake experience caused him to question how God might save him. Further destabilizing his young life, at age seventeen, he was drafted for mandatory military service, although he was not sent to the front during World War I. Immediately after the war, his father remarried, making family life even more miserable.

---

[97] 7.1 magnitude, killing between 75,000 to 200,000 lives.

Tony determined he would leave for America at his first opportunity to seek his fortune in the New World. That same year, at age twenty-one, Tony obtained his passage to America when someone else dropped out at the last minute, causing him to scramble in getting a passport, ticket, and traveling to the port—all within twenty-three hours. With little in his pocket but great optimism, he left Sicily.

A New Life in the New World

When he arrived in New York, he had only one address of an Italian family who lived there. He had no connections there with family or friends. He didn't even understand or speak English. Yet Tony obtained both lodging and a steady job on his first day in America. Six months after arriving in America, he purchased his first car and went into the taxi business. After building his taxi business to three cars, he purchased an additional expensive luxury car to obtain a chauffeur job at an extraordinarily high rate of $450 per month. On the side, Tony partnered with his brother Joe, who had eventually joined him in New York, to sell eggs. This new business gradually developed into a grocery store.

During this time, a young man applied to Tony's grocery store for an errand job. His name was Santo Consiglio, and he would become a longtime employee and good friend. The store also attracted another individual who would become very important in his life: Florence Stark. Tony—also called Nino at that time—was enthralled with this Protestant woman named

Florence. She frequently went to the store. So frequently, in fact, that they eventually married.

Transformation Begins

One success followed another: Tony became one of the first New York entrepreneurs to open a self-serve grocery store featuring fresh fruits and produce—the precursor of today's self-serve supermarkets.

In the late 1930s, he sold the grocery store, and the couple moved to Florida in hopes of starting a farm. While preparing to move, Tony spent time researching at the New York Public Library. Here, he found an unshelved book entitled *The Life of Christ.* From reading this book, Tony became passionate about reading the Bible directly, something his Roman Catholic upbringing in Sicily had discouraged. While exploring the Bible, Tony became fascinated with a concept he discovered about Jesus giving eternal salvation as a gift. This was liberating news to Tony, who up to that time had doubted he could ever be good enough to earn or qualify for heaven.

His first big proof of God's personal care was the one year they spent in Virginia raising tomatoes before moving to Florida. Tony prayed for a $5,000 profit. The harvest looked more abundant, but Tony could not hire enough workers, so much of the crop failed. His wife calculated their net profit after harvest to find they had earned exactly $5,000.00!

Settling in Bradenton, Florida, Tony heard about a local

cafeteria for sale. He spontaneously purchased it with nearly everything he possessed at the time—cash, borrowing against the farm and his car, selling the remainder of his New York businesses, etc. He further borrowed to make renovations while focusing on serving the freshest meals. Before long, he envisioned opening other restaurants, starting with the Terrace Restaurant in Miami. During World War II, the paltry number of tourists in Miami made it difficult to earn a profit, so against his better judgment, Tony agreed to serve alcohol. However, he felt God would not honor this decision. On the verge of losing the Miami restaurant, he received a large offer from a local nightclub owner to buy it.

After selling the restaurant, he started a citrus gift box company in Miami. Sales grew so rapidly that they moved back to Bradenton to acquire a warehouse and plant while their friends continued to sell gift boxes for them in Miami. The new company, Fruit Industries, Inc.,[98] would gradually focus on selling to New York hotels and restaurants with the help of his old employee and friend, Santo Consiglio. Everyone expected the fruit to spoil on the way to New York, but Tony designed a refrigeration truck with extra ice packing to keep the fruit juice fresh—particularly orange juice. Demand soared in New York and Boston, causing explosive growth in the company, which was a challenging situation to manage. The company expanded to fifty employees as sales continued to increase to a critical management point.

Tony asked for God's guidance on what to do. He prayed for

---

[98] Formed in 1947.

days, including praying while driving around town on business. On one of these trips, he noticed a local motel named Tropicana. He immediately felt led to change the name and logo of his company to Tropicana, Inc. Around this same time, Tony took a huge risk in ordering $1 million worth of trucks and building a new processing plant. To celebrate the completion of the project, he generously started the first annual employee gala to thank employees for their help. But less than an hour after all employees left the party, his new plant burned to the ground: Defective workmanship on the tar roof had sparked a fire in the hot Florida sun. Tony trusted in God to help him recover quickly. Thankfully, nobody was hurt.

Sadly, Tony would soon become a widower. In 1951, Florence suddenly became ill and died. Tony lived alone for eight years. During this time, his maid Mary kept his house and made meals. He treated her much better than Southern whites did during that era towards blacks, helping her and her family.

One of his employees invited him to a Bible study in nearby Saratoga. At that Bible study, where he saw many of his friends from his Methodist church founders group, Tony learned about the Bible's message that he could be certain he would go to heaven. This provided such relief that he vowed to share this insight with everyone he could.

He was also passionate about school nutrition. Early on in the formation of his Tropicana company, he pioneered the inclusion of Florida's citrus juices in school meal programs to help improve children's health. Tony patented a pasteurization process in 1954 that allowed safe bottling of orange juice without refrigeration. Company sales reached levels well beyond what Tony originally expected: Just as he had trusted, God provided the right people to help him manage the company and expand its reach across the entire nation.

During this period, Tony decided he could only marry again if it was to a missionary. Again, he trusted in God. And God provided. Tony met Sanna Barlow, who had recently returned from the South African mission field, at their local church. The couple was married in 1954.

During the 1950s and 60s, Tony invested in a Protestant church and radio ministry in his native Sicily. His ambition was to bring the liberating truths he discovered in the Bible to his family still in Italy, friends, and anyone who would listen. He even began preaching in churches and evangelizing to open-air groups.

Transforming Orange Juice, Tankers, and Trains

Tony continued to innovate, including buying a tanker he converted into a 1.5 million gallon carrier of fresh orange juice. This tanker, which he named the S.S. Tropicana, operated from the only Atlantic deep water port in Florida, built by Tony to have a port capable of handling his growing business needs. The tanker allowed him to ship directly at a lower cost than rail or truck transport to New York City, turning around shipments in under one week.

Innovation did not stop there. During a bad frost year, he

created one of the world's first floating fruit processing plants: It processed Mexican oranges into juice and then transported it to Bradenton. This floating processing plant increased the amount of juice obtained from Mexican orange growers at a much cheaper cost. The process Tony used eliminated the bulky room and weight of transporting skins, seeds, and other parts of the unprocessed orange. Tony also developed and patented a method for freezing pure whole citrus juice into blocks for storage and shipping, enabling people in many far-off places to enjoy fresh citrus juices for the first time. Less creative competitors could not compete with Tony's Tropicana.

Even after selling his company in 1978, Tony continued to innovate because he wanted to continue bringing refreshment and jobs to as many people as possible. For example, in 1980, he created "The Great Snow White Train"—a mile-long orange juice concentrate carrier to bring fresh orange juice to the Northeastern United States at a lower cost than either trucking or ship. He received many patents for his creativity.

In 1973, in honor of his contributions to American enterprise and society. President Nixon invited him to a White House dinner. The invitation brought even greater recognition to his company.

Transformation Till the End

In 1976, several criminals violently ransacked his home. Fortunately, Tony and his wife just missed the invasion and emerged unscathed, as did the household staff. This prompted Tony to meditate on the 23rd Psalm and consider how the Lord is his Shepherd, who enabled him to do more of God's work.

In response to these theological reflections, Tony began plans to sell the company and embark upon a second career—philanthropy: Two years later, Tony sold Tropicana to Beatrice Foods for half a billion dollars. By that time, the company employed more than 8,000 people, and profits during his last decade of ownership had increased 82 percent.

He then founded the Aurora Foundation to engage in various charitable works—particularly in bringing the Gospel message to both America and his native Italy. Throughout the time he spent building Tropicana and leading the Aurora Foundation, Tony had been taking annual trips back to Italy to preach, support, and encourage mission work and distribute Bibles.

His efforts caused both Forbes and Fortune magazines to feature him on the front cover. Despite the media fanfare, Tony was not particularly interested in the additional fame this brought him. He was more excited to build an affordable village for returning missionaries of any denomination who lacked the funds to retire or buy a home.

He received many awards for his pioneering work in agriculture and was inducted into the Florida Agricultural Hall of

Fame in 1987. For both his contributions to the citrus industry and his humanitarian efforts, Tony received an honorary doctorate from the University of Tampa in 1980. Locally, he became known as "Mr. Tropicana."

Upon building his missionary retirement village in Florida, he turned his attention to another big project. At the age of eighty, Tony launched the Bible Alliance to produce cassette tapes of Bible books for the blind. Working in partnership with the Billy Graham Crusade staff, he built a financially self-sustaining worldwide ministry in multiple languages. Under his leadership, they grew to a staff of twenty, headed by his nephew Joe Aleppo and his nephew's wife, Georgia. Today, this foundation continues Tony's work with its $19 million income to support many new church plantings, mission conferences, a seminary, and other evangelism efforts worldwide.

God's presence and favor were evident through Tony's life—in the way God spared his life and blessed his repentance with awards and great success in both his business and charitable activities. Tony trusted God, and God provided.

18

God's Employee, Humility, and Plastic

"Christ is the answer."
— *The Stanita Foundation Building*

Stanley Tam

1915-current

Entrepreneurs are often known for their strong self-confidence and ego. It's part of what enables their success. However, Christian entrepreneurs frequently commit to crediting the majority of their success back to God, and are encouraged by their Christian faith to practice the virtue of humility, even in the face of great personal blessings. This chapter highlights a man who sacrificed everything to God, living as an employee rather than a steward of God's bounty—Stanley Tam.

Two great events early in Stanley Tam's life have affected his outlook throughout his long adult life. As a teenager and young adult, Stanley observed his parents struggle through the Great Depression. His parents' trials convinced him to become a successful entrepreneur, and not be dependent upon the graces of an employer. Upon graduating high school in 1933, he immediately took a job as a door-to-door salesman for Stanley Home Products.[99]

Stanley's family had always attended church regularly, but he did not feel personally connected to Christ. Then, one day, while he was demonstrating household items to a farmer's wife, she talked to him about how Jesus could transform his life. Six weeks after talking with that farmer's wife, he accepted Jesus as his personal Savior and vowed to share that personal transformation with other people.

Transforming Silver and Plastics

In 1936—using twenty-five dollars he had saved along with a similar capital contribution from an inventor partner—Stanley started his first company. It was started during the worst part of the Great Depression, lasting from 1929-1933. He named the company the States Smelting and Refining Corporation. The intention was to extract abandoned silver, but like so many start-ups, they learned to quickly pivot when opportunities presented themselves. Stanley noticed an opportunity: Eastman Kodak Company, which commanded over 90 percent of the film sales market, used an emulsion

---

[99] Stanley also briefly held a job running a gas filling station but was fired for filing a report a day or so late.

on its photographic film, which included silver halide salts and gelatin coating. Kodak used approximately twenty tons of silver per week to develop that emulsion, 80 percent of which was rinsed away during the film development process. Working with his inventor partner, who created a silver reclaiming machine, Stanley developed a clever way to extract the silver at a minimal cost.

He made agreements with photography studios and with the inventor to set up royalty agreements from placing the machines in the studios. At the same time, Stanley concentrated on building marketing channels to sell the silver. The business was a creative idea, but the cost of distributing the devices became a burden. The crushing point came when the Internal Revenue Service demanded a 50 percent tax on silver. The IRS eventually settled the dispute for a few hundred dollars, admitting the initial assessment was wrong. However, the resolution came too late to prevent the business from failing, due to an inability to meet both the onerous tax burden and creditor obligations in a timely manner. That the business was started during the worst part of the Great Depression was the final blow.

On the trip back home from this failure, Stanley felt God reaffirm Stanley's desire to become a business success and call him to become a partner with God—utilizing future profits to share the Gospel. Stanley promised to give God the credit for any future success.

In the midst of this financial turmoil, Stanley married

Juanita[100] in 1939. For their honeymoon, they traveled in a house trailer for six weeks down to Texas and back, selling silver recovery to every photography business they could find. At this point, marriage was a true leap of faith for both of them. Juanita was supportive, and they trusted God to see them through their financial difficulties. They were a well-suited pair: Juanita was the one who thought of setting up a mail-order service rather than personally delivering and picking up each silver collection device, enabling company sales to soar.

After his first business failed, all Stanley possessed was his original $25 initial investment. To add to this, his father lent another $12 to launch Stanley's next company—United States Plastic Corporation in Lima, Ohio. In this second business, Stanley used plastic buckets. The first synthetic plastic, or polymer, was invented in 1869. Plastics were applied to various new uses starting in the early 1900s, exploding into everyday usage in nearly every type of manufactured product after World War II. Ever the visionary, Stanley recognized the future potential of plastic. So, with a $37 capital stake, he started a plastics manufacturing company.

Stanley kept his promise to God. As the company grew and his business travels took him to many locations, he always devoted time to sharing the Bible message with other business people and individuals he met during his travels. The first three years were a struggle, as he traveled to thirty states building the business. Keeping costs as low as possible and

---

[100] 1916-2006

expanding wherever possible, the company gradually grew substantially.

In 1940, consistent with his promise to God, Stanley set up the Stanita Foundation, a tax-exempt charity, to own 51 percent of the plastics company. Fifty-one percent of the dividends were donated directly to Christian missions, making God the senior partner in the firm. Over time, Stanley contributed over $100 million from that initial $37 start for Christian mission efforts—a phenomenal return on investment!

Giving All to God

On a trip through several nations in South America during 1955, Stanley again felt God calling him towards a greater commitment. Rather than partners, Stanley felt called to become God's employee, turning over 100 percent of his company to God's ownership. Juanita immediately and eagerly supported this decision. Together they signed over 100 percent of the company's stock to the Stanita Foundation, then quickly made plans to accommodate the expansion God would bring. They built a plant four times larger than the old one, consisting of five acres of floor space, located on a curve in interstate seventy-five, highly visible from the highway. On the side of the building, it still says today, "Christ is the answer." That same year, Stanley developed an electric silver collector, which included a plastic bucket. Customers began expressing more interest in the new plastic buckets than the silver extraction.

What solidified sales and trust in the company's growing

line of products was his reaction to an innocent error that a customer rapidly spread around the business community. A silver processing company had accidentally paid $3,000 more than the value of the quantity extracted. Stanley notified the company owner and returned the $3,000 out of a $5,000 payment (60 percent of the money paid, which Stanley really needed for his expenses). His action built significant credibility with the customer and all the people that customer told the story to.

The rapidly expanding demand for plastic products fueled enormous growth in the company's sales. Stanley was reminded of the parable of the man who sold everything to obtain the pearl of great price.[101] His building project followed this wisdom, but it was not easy. The cash flow did not initially support such a great and expensive leap of faith. To make matters worse, a building subcontractor forced a dispute. Stanley still paid the subcontractor's bill, even though he was not legally obligated to do so, in order to financially help the subcontractor.

Stanley hasn't stopped at donating huge sums for evangelism and discipleship. He has given countless talks to a wide variety of audiences worldwide and has written four books:

- God Owns My Business (1969)
- God's Woodshed: The Power of a Cleansed Life (1991)
- Stanley Tam's Incredible Adventures with God (2002)

---

[101] Matthew 13:45-46.

- Every Christian a Soul Winner (2010)

Over time, many people came to discover Stanley's story. Today a significant number of people still stop at the plant to hear about how God can own a company and how a commitment to engage in marketplace ministry through a business can work in practice. Stanley's gentle discussions and concern for others led an average of three people daily to Jesus through nearly all of his adult life. Through Stanley's efforts, nearly 1-1/2 million people have accepted Jesus as their personal savior and have had their lives transformed.

Stanley received an honorary doctorate for his commitment to discipling others. Many churches in developing nations were founded due to Stanley, whose focus was on both learning about and sharing God's Word whenever possible. He strove to honor God through the business, from including Gospel tract information in every product shipment to talking with vendors, employees, and even people walking in off the street about God.

The company started a Christian radio station and produced evangelistic films in addition to sharing his personal witness to others, stopping work to counsel others, asking for his help, sending tracts to customers, and funding many new churches and ministries worldwide.

In his personal walk with God, Stanley invested a significant amount of time every day in personal Bible study, as well as leading his family and business associates to understand the Bible more thoroughly. He was noted for his close walk with

God and obedience to God's leading. This individual effort led to several mass ministries. For example, on a trip to Korea, he became acquainted with the Oriental Mission Society. This organization had the goal of sharing the Bible throughout the former Japanese Empire. Stanley offered to fund this evangelistic society to reach all the people of Japan with the Bible, resulting in thousands of Japanese coming to Christ and the founding of 400 churches.

Stanley looked ahead to envision how his passion for sharing what Jesus has done for him with many people at least a century in the future and further. In his low-key way, Stanley gave back everything he owned to God, creating a perpetual funding mechanism for evangelism which continues to provide outreach. Utilizing his entrepreneurial experience, Stanley demanded budgets and other accountability tools for evangelistic results. He has been a major donor to OMS International, Inc., Every Community for Christ, and many other evangelism ministries. And he always requires decisive action and accountability.

Yet, Stanley is perhaps not well known because, throughout his life, he always kept the focus on God and the Great Commission, avoiding calling attention to himself. His family never thought of themselves as materially rich because Stanley set a modest salary for himself back in the early 1950s so materialism would not tempt him or his family away from maintaining their focus on God's Word. In retirement, Stanley runs a small woodworking shop and continues to share his faith and life testimony in his community, especially groups of teenagers and business owners. He challenges fellow entrepreneurs to seek opportunities to share God's message through their businesses.

Exercising the virtue of humility, Stanley recognized his shyness held back his sales ability. His family history of business failures by his grandfather, father, and then himself confirmed he had no special aptitude for business. However, a heart for God and total commitment to follow Jesus were the crucial difference that gave him such enormous success. In other words, Stanley considered himself proof and an example that if he could be successful by following God, then anyone else can do the same also.

19

Overcoming Bias to Empower Women

"I think the biggest legacy we are going to leave is a whole community of children who believe they can do anything in this world because they watched their mamas do it."
— Mary Kay Ash

Mary Kay Ash

1918-2001

Women also make great entrepreneurs, as the following story illustrates. Mary Kay Wagner was born to a poor family near Houston, Texas, just six months before the end of World War I. Growing up, she had to take care of her sickly dad when he returned from a sanatorium. She learned to cook at age seven and received much encouragement from her hard-working mother who always told her "You can do it!" for everything she tried. At seventeen,[102] she married Ben Rogers, with whom she

---

[102] 1935

had two sons and a daughter. Ben was a local radio personality during the Depression until he was drafted into the Army to serve overseas in World War II. During the war, Mary Kay sold encyclopedias door to door and she became quite successful. When Ben returned from combat, he asked for a divorce after running off with another woman, which left her devastated and very poor, as she tried to raise three young children.

Mary Kay quickly rallied, however, finding work with Stanley Home Products from 1945 to 1952 selling housewares and cleaning supplies. She then took a job at World Gift Company. Within ten years, she extended the company's distribution network into forty-three states and became a unit manager. Mary was frustrated and discouraged, but most of all she was enraged. She, a top sales producer, was passed over for promotion because she was a woman. The management promoted a man she had trained, and made him her new supervisor at twice her pay.

This caused her to "retire" at age forty-five with the intention of writing a book for women on how they could enter the business world. By this point, she had moved to Dallas. About this same time, after spending nearly half her life up to that point as a single mother, she married for the second time to George Hallenbeck, who encouraged her efforts. Mary Kay's book morphed into a business plan to start Beauty by Mary Kay. However, only a couple months after their marriage, while George was working on developing financial models for her new business only one month before its opening, he had a sudden heart attack and passed away.

Transforming Female Entrepreneurship

This was a time in history when women were discouraged from working outside the home, and when they did find work, they were mostly low-level secretarial-type positions. The majority of women were discouraged from obtaining college degrees, and women's opinions were not taken seriously by the business world.

Mary was shaken, but she was determined to support herself financially and help other women in similar positions, despite the discouraging advice from her lawyer and accountant not to try without her husband. Instead of giving up, Mary Kay borrowed $5,000 from her older son, Richard, and risked everything she owned to launch the new company. To mitigate risk, she asked her younger son, Ben, to join her in Dallas to help her launch the new company in a very small office. She asked Ben to take the place of her recently deceased husband as the business and financial manager for the fledgling firm. Mary Kay had also recruited nine friends to help her sell beauty products.

Her first product was a skin softener she used herself and thought would be helpful to other women. Mary Kay purchased the recipe from the woman who had developed it and contracted with a local manufacturer to produce the product, expanding into an entire line of skincare products based upon this formula. She planned to use a direct sales approach—one of the few non-clerical opportunities open to women at the time—just as she had throughout her career.

However, Mary Kay developed a unique take on the sales approach that no direct sales company had yet tried: She called her sales staff consultants and taught them to demonstrate the product without any high-pressure sales pitches. She believed once women saw how the products improved their appearances, the products would sell themselves, and women would appreciate the educational and consultative "no pressure" approach.

Results spoke for themselves. During the first quarter in business, her little company sold $34,000 in products. The following year they sold $198,000. The second full year in business sales boomed to $800,000 with a mushrooming sales force exceeding 3,000 part-time and full-time consultants. Ever the optimist and eager to instill her infectious enthusiasm into other women to boost their confidence and sense of self-worth, Mary Kay stopped selling products herself so she could concentrate on motivating and training her sales force.

Initially, the company had sold wigs along with beauty products but quickly dropped the wigs. Mary Kay experimented with sales techniques, which swiftly caused her to close the storefront retail shop, offering products solely through direct sales by her consultants. Following the concept of using parties that she learned from Stanley Home Products, Mary Kay trained consultants to set up parties in offices and homes. The emphasis was never on sales but instead on teaching skincare. Many sales professionals doubted this approach could work.

She proved them wrong.

The company eventually settled on promoting home parties. They found that home situations gave women an opportunity to try products before purchasing, and do so in a private setting. This was preferable to many women over removing their makeup in a public store with strangers walking by or in front of male co-workers in an office. Mary Kay also found that keeping parties to a maximum of six women kept it intimate and manageable for the hostess.

Mary Kay kept the product line focused—starting with a basic kit of just a few products. In fact, over the next thirty-eight years, the product line consisted of only about forty items. Working sixteen-hour days with both of her sons during the first year, she earned enough to support herself and invest in a larger office. She and her family held the first "Seminar" for consultants close to their first anniversary.

The Seminar included a mixture of education, motivation, relaxing fun, and family-care ideas. She wanted to recognize consultants' contributions to the company growth through the seminar and help them in their personal and professional lives. Company songs have always been an important part of the annual Seminar since that first year. Mary Kay believed songs provide an esprit de corps, particularly when accompanied with clapping, stomping, and other actions.

Transforming Incentives

Another radical innovation she pioneered was to provide incentives to both customers and sales staff alike. Customers could obtain free products by hosting a party, purchasing a certain volume of products, or encouraging friends to purchase products. Sales consultants received generous rewards based upon sales volume rather than profit margins. Mary Kay gave away family vacations, jewelry, and most famously, pink Cadillacs to the top performers. The pink Cadillac giveaways started in 1969, only six years after launching the company. By 1994 she had given away more than $ 100 million of pink Cadillacs, and the Mary Kay fleet is today the largest commercial fleet of General Motors cars in the world.

In case you are wondering where the idea of the pink Cadillacs came from, Mary Kay had a pink bathroom, which inspired the start of the emphasis on pink, even though her personal cars were not always pink.

In 1966—three years after founding what would become Mary Kay Cosmetics, Inc.—she married again, for the last time: Melville J. Ash was another supportive and encouraging man. While Mel did not take an active part in the company, he encouraged and supported her efforts. For example, Mary and Mel would host the top producers in their home, during the annual Mary Kay Seminars. They enjoyed fourteen years together until his death from lung cancer.

Mary Kay instituted a policy for headquarters staff which was and still is exceedingly rare in the corporate world. All employees are expected to be courteous and responsive to consultants whenever they visit corporate headquarters. This included all top executives and even Mary Kay herself, when she was alive. Any consultant can ask any question from anyone at the corporate offices and receive a prompt, accurate, and courteous reply. How many CEOs and executives in other companies even acknowledge the people who fund their salaries? Mary Kay wanted to make her consultants feel highly valued.

The company continued meteoric growth. In 1968, the company went public only five years after starting. Against advice from lawyers, accountants, and other professional advisers, she and her son Richard privatized the company in 1985, which proved to be a wise move leading to massive additional profit growth. But this was not why they retook full ownership. Public stockholders and analysts began questioning the necessity of lavish rewards for consultants, particularly the pink Cadillacs. Knowing these were important for motivating consultants and wishing to give women a sense of special accomplishment, Mary Kay decided it was more important to return public shareholder money than to reduce her consultants' motivation and reward system.

In 1987, at sixty-nine, Mary Kay retired from active management but retained the title and active board participation as Chairwoman, continuing to come into work until her stroke in 1996, when she retired entirely. She retained the title of Chairwoman Emeritus until her death. By 1993 the company exceeded $1 billion in sales with nearly 400,000 independent beauty consultants in twenty nations, becoming the largest direct seller of skincare products in the United States.

Throughout her life, Mary Kay believed in giving back to God from the blessings He sent her way. For example, when her church decided to add a youth addition to their building, Mary Kay promised to match the church members contributions dollar for dollar in a single day after their fund drive. She did this despite the fact that her company was in its early years and therefore minimally profitable. Mary Kay believed strongly in leading her company according to Biblical principles. Consultants receive time management training that includes not only business issues but also advice on care for their families, including their husbands. There are workshops for husbands to build their appreciation and support for their wives. The company also offers seminars for both consultants and their husbands, on building stronger, happier marriages and families. Mary Kay included all of this in order to strengthen marriages and promote a healthy balance between a consultant's personal and professional lives.

Mary and Mel enjoyed fourteen years together until his death from lung cancer. She funded the Mary Kay Ash Center for Cancer Immunotherapy Research at St. Paul Medical Center in Dallas. In 1993, she attended the dedication of this medical center. In 1996 she established the Mary Kay Ash Charitable Foundation[103] to support cancer research, particularly cancer that disproportionately affects women, and combat domestic violence. She asked staff and consultants to join her while funding the Foundation with many millions of dollars.

---

[103] Now renamed the Mary Kay Foundation.

She also frequently supported church and other charity efforts, in addition to creating jobs for 475,000 employees plus over 500,000 independent consultants around the world.

Mary Kay had a gift for motivating and uplifting women. She would frequently encourage them with these inspirational lines:

- *I created this company for you.*
- *At Mary Kay, you are in business for yourself, not by yourself.*
- *God didn't have time to make a nobody. As a result, you can have or be anything you want.*
- *Pretend that every single person you meet has a sign around his or her neck that says "Make Me Feel Important." Not only will you succeed in business, you will succeed in life.*

As further inspiration for her consultants and all women, Mary Kay published three books. Her first book was an autobiography entitled *Mary Kay*,[104] which sold more than a million copies. Her second book, *Mary Kay on People Management*,[105] explained her philosophy of respect and care, particularly for women in the business world. Her final book, *Mary Kay: You Can Have It All*,[106] was intended as a motivational book for women discouraged over their lives or wondering how to handle family and life challenges.

Mary Kay's company philosophy includes three pillars:

---

[104] 1981

[105] 1984

[106] 1995

- Golden Rule—cheerfully helping others without expectation of return, even if a new consultant is not part of a director's network.
- Right priorities—God first, family second, career third.
- Belief in the beautiful potential inside every human being, given enough encouragement and praise.

Fortune Magazine listed her company as among the top one hundred fastest-growing companies for over twenty years consecutively. Both Fortune and Forbes magazines also listed her among the top one hundred best companies to work for.

In keeping with the Biblical principle that God created both men and women as equals, Mary Kay opened the business world and unlimited earnings potential for all women. Despite the hardships she endured throughout her life, she achieved her dream of providing opportunities for women that she had initially been denied. She gave millions of women the ability to successfully raise families and provide for them by being their own bosses—setting their own levels of achievements and work schedules, so they can truly "have it all." Perhaps this can best be summarized from a quote she gave sometime after her retirement. When asked what she considered her greatest achievement, she proudly replied, "I think the biggest legacy we are going to leave is a whole community of children who believe they can do anything in this world because they watched their mamas do it."

20

Value, Respect, and the Chicken Sandwich

"Total commitment is not instant success,
but it does insulate the entrepreneur from most discouragement
and from quitting.
Commitment also allows the Christian to see God helping you."
— *Truett Cathy*

Truett Cathy

1921-2014

All of the stories up to this point include clear indications that Christian entrepreneurs believe in showing respect for others and providing substantial value to customers. This next story illustrates a Christian tycoon whose company is noted more for these qualities than the products sold. Samuel Truett Cathy, better known as Truett Cathy—he rarely used his first name—was born in Eatonton, Georgia, a tiny town almost halfway between Atlanta and Augusta. Since his family was so poor, his mother ran a boarding house to support Truett and his sisters during the Great Depression. To help his struggling family, he assisted his mother in the kitchen and was taught to cook by her.

In his early twenties, he served in the Army during World War II. Three years after returning from the war, he married his childhood sweetheart, Jeannette,[107] whom he met at age eight at church. They had three biological children. All of them eventually got involved in the family business. During their sixty-five-year marriage, they also sponsored many foster children.

Total Commitment

In 1946, Truett started a restaurant called Dwarf House Grill in a suburb of Atlanta not far from the airport. At age twenty-five, Truett sold his car and borrowed $6,000, which was 150 percent of his net worth at the time—a considerable risk—to fund his business. The business had a very slow start, so he and his then partner and his brother Ben started giving away free food samples to workers as they drove past the restaurant. Truett remarked on those early years:

> *Total commitment is not instant success, but it does insulate the entrepreneur from most discouragement and from quitting. Commitment also allows the Christian to see God helping you.*

---

[107] 1924–2016

Many of his early customers came from the nearby Ford automobile plant and Delta Airlines employees on their way to or from work. The Dwarf House was a small restaurant with a limited menu. Truitt's approach was to start very small with what they could afford while still maintaining big dreams. The giveaways of free samples soon attracted many customers, especially from the two large employers nearby. Working very long hours, the partners kept the restaurant open twenty-four hours for six days per week to service all three shifts at the Ford plant.

Shortly after opening this restaurant, Truett noticed a changing trend in customer food tastes. Chickens were cheaper than steak, which appealed to his sense of frugality. However, some blood often stayed on the chicken bone, causing customers to mistakenly believe the chicken was not fully cooked. Truett also took note from his Delta customers that airlines began serving boneless chicken to keep down costs.

Goode Brothers Poultry supplied Delta Airlines. Truett contacted Goode to purchase their leftover scrap pieces, which cooked very fast with no remaining blood stain problems. When removing the skin, that also removed much of the flavor, so he experimented with recipes to restore it. Truett often offered free samples of his experiments to his customers to get their reactions. After just a couple of years, customers helped him refine a unique and hard-to-duplicate flavor. Over the next twenty-one years, Truett would open a number of Dwarf House restaurants around the Atlanta metropolitan area, focusing increasingly on chicken rather than other meats.

In 1964, he attended the Southeastern Restaurant Trade Association convention, cooking samples for other restaurant owners in hopes of licensing his chicken sandwich to them. Over fifty restaurants and several hotels signed up. This quick success caused him to consider developing a franchising model rather than licensing to expand more rapidly and assure high-quality control over his product to the customer.

In 1967, Truett was ready to launch his second restaurant, which he could now afford to open himself without any partner money. He named it Chick-fil-A, Inc. That name was a key to his success: The name clearly conveyed that he sold chicken fillets. As a bonus, the name could be trademarked to prevent competition from conveying anything similar, thus providing a significant marketing advantage. The focus of the entire organization was a quickly made and unique chicken sandwich. He used pressure cookers to cook a chicken breast in under four minutes, sealing in the juices, eliminating warming cabinets, and allowing time for hand breading every piece.

Truett opened the first restaurant under the Chick-fil-A name in Atlanta's first shopping mall. This was before malls became popular and even prior to the invention of the mall food court: So he was the only restaurant. His timing was perfect. In 1970, beef consumption dropped 15 percent while poultry doubled over the next thirty years, according to the United States Department of Agriculture. The initial mall locations were followed by stand-alone restaurants. Truitt's insight rode the wave of consumer demand for chicken at the beginning of the surge in demand. That success was then compounded by the franchise model for opening new locations, quickly scaling the tiny restaurant chain from six restaurants in 1970 to 958 by 2000.

In 2008, Truitt opened a new restaurant, Upscale Pizza, in Fayetteville, Georgia, but his business focus still remained on leading Chick-fil-A. In contrast to current "best practices" thinking at many companies, Truitt did not plan beyond an eight-month window. Truitt wanted the flexibility to take advantage of unexpected opportunities.

A Culture of Kindness

According to Truitt, the key to Chick-fil-A's success was keeping everything simple and low cost. To this day, corporate emphasis has always been on the main chicken sandwich. The menu and operations processes have been consistent for over sixty years. A critical component to its success is high-quality on-site leadership for each franchisee. No absentee ownership is tolerated.

Franchisees are taught to treat customers and employees with love, following the Biblical Golden Rule to do unto others as you would have them do unto you. Cheerful attitudes are encouraged by restaurant managers and at national training. Employees are expected to respond to any customer compliment with "my pleasure." More than 70 percent of those employees are teenagers, and overwhelmingly Christians. In both training materials and by leadership example, corporate officers and franchisees are expected to model and teach a servant leadership and hospitality mindset throughout the organization to every employee.

This attitude is so pervasive, it provides a distinctive dining atmosphere that makes even the chain's strongest critics often inclined to dine there. At times people picketing the company's support for traditional Christian and American values have purchased meals from the restaurants or occasionally been treated by compassionate franchisees to a free drink or snack. Truett emphasized "second-mile" service such as table flowers, fresh ground pepper, and toilet paper folded like in a hotel. These services are nearly absent in competing fast-food restaurants.

That culture of kindness is contagious. On occasion, employees have been observed to change a customer's flat tire, return lost keys or phone by driving the lost items to their owner's office or home, and even buy a customer a Christmas meal. Truett developed a giveaway item called Be Our Guest Card. This is an invitation to try a specific Chick-fil-A item for free. The card not only helps establish new franchisees in a new market, but it also gives employees personal contact with potential customers.

Company philosophy, ingrained into every franchisee and employee, can be summarized in the following eight principles:

- Start as early as possible
- Avoid debt
- Observe what works for others
- Set priorities
- Expand cautiously but continuously

- Be prepared for disappointments
- Courtesy is cheap but brings great dividends
- Invite God to be involved in every decision

Jeannette, Truitt's wife, also worked in the original Dwarf House restaurants. The couple's eldest son Dan is now chairman of the company. On the company website, Dan stated:

> *Our mother has always been the spiritual nucleus and encourager of our family. I can't remember a day when she was not in full support of Dad in his work and vision for the Chick-fil-A business.*

Both Truett and Jeannette were determined to lead their company by Biblical principles. For example, all stores and the corporate headquarters have always stayed closed on Sundays so staff could attend church and have a relaxing day with their families.

All while growing his business, Truett taught Sunday School classes—for more than half a century. He was interested in Christian business education, writing five books himself, co-authoring a sixth book, and contributing to two others. The book titles are instructive as to his Christian worldview and topics he wished to share widely:

- *It's Easier to Succeed than to Fail*[108] was a motivational book.
- *Eat more Chikin: Inspire More People*[109] was Truett's auto-

---

[108] 1989

[109] 2002

biography.
- *It's Better to Build Boys than Mend Men*[110] explored his ideas on parenting.
- *How Did You Do It, Truett?*[111] explained his business success.
- *Wealth, Is It Worth It?*[112] explained the significance of money in today's society.
- *What My Parents Did Right*[113] was an anthology he contributed to.
- *Conversations on Success*[114] was a collection of stories he contributed to.
- *Generosity Factor: Discover the Joy of Giving Your Time, Talent, and Treasure*[115] was a book he co-authored with Ken Blanchard, a successful management expert and author of *The One Minute Manager*.

Truett sponsored the college Peach Bowl, now known as the Chick-fil-A Bowl. He established a Leadership Scholarship program for his employees, which has awarded more than $23 million in $1,000 scholarships over the past thirty-five years. Truett gave so generously of his time and money that, among numerous awards and honorary doctorates, in 2008, he received both the William E. Simon Prize for Philanthropic Leadership and the President's Lifetime Volunteer Service

---

[110] 2004

[111] 2007

[112] 2011

[113] 2002

[114] 2003

[115] 2010

Award[116] from United States President George W. Bush.

In 2002, he was invited to address a Congressional committee on business ethics lapses. His focus was Proverbs 22:1:

> *A good name is rather to be chosen than great riches*
> *and loving favor rather than silver and gold.*

He told Congressional leaders that businesses have no ethics and are not dishonest either. Only individuals do and are. Business success is a reflection of the leader's character. You should live consistent with your convictions. Product, people, and purpose all fit together.

His restaurants consistently generate greater sales in six days than competitors do in all seven days, while his company gives its employees a day of rest every week. Management treats employees like family. Though thousands apply to become franchisees, they open only one hundred stores per year to assure quality control in selecting and training the best franchisees. As a result, the company has less than five percent operator turnover—an exceptionally low turnover rate among fast-food chains.

Truett believed in delegating most details and trusting both managers and employees to act in an ethical, Biblical manner. He instead emphasized building relationships that last for the very long term with managers, vendors, employees, customers, the community, and everyone they could serve.

---

[116] Also known as the President's Call to Service Award.

This still is the company's approach to ethics which he shared with Congress: It cannot be legislated, it can only be modeled.

Unlike some of the other Christian entrepreneurs featured in this book, Truett did not explicitly seek to utilize his company as a ministry platform. However, it is common for employees, franchisees, and executives to share their faith with customers and other people when there is an opportunity to do so. Some franchisees have Bible tracts available if customers wish to read any. Instead of explicitly trying to conduct ministry efforts at each restaurant, Truett and his associates apply faith principles to the business operations. For example, franchise operators pay a very small $5,000 deposit, then 15 percent of sales for marketing and operations support,[117] but split net profits 50 percent. This shifts part of the risk to the company.[118] This approach also creates motivation to both generate sales and manage operations efficiently.

Truett was noted for listening actively to all operators and employees. For headquarters support staff, he was frequently known to exclaim, "If you're not selling chicken, you'd better be supporting someone who is!" Officer and board retreats begin with personal sharing and prayer time. He encouraged franchisees to become involved in giving back to the community and wanted them to donate many Be Our Guest cards to nearby schools, churches, and civic organizations.

---

[117] This is far less than the million-dollar entrance fees some other fast-food chains charge.

[118] Unlike other franchises, which take a percentage of revenues, so franchisee location expenses do not affect their income.

Perhaps Truett's purposes that he gave to the two major organizations he founded summarize his efforts as a Christian entrepreneur. In the corporate headquarters, a plaque in the lobby announces the corporate purpose to everyone:

> *Chick-fil-A's corporate purpose is to glorify God by being a faithful steward of all that is entrusted to us, to have a positive influence on all who come in contact with Chick-fil-A.*

In 1984, he launched the WinShape Foundation to help young people become winners in life. In addition to offering scholarships, grants, and other financial support, the Foundation provides six major ministries, conducted at its Mt. Berry Georgia campus and throughout the United States:

- Youth summer camps providing character development.
- Providing group foster homes for high-risk children.
- Team-building and servant leadership development programs.
- Guidance for strengthening all stages of marriage.
- College degree—in conjunction with Barry College—in Christian servant leadership.
- Restorative retreats for couples and organizations at the Foundation's retreat center.

The Foundation's ministry goal is:

> *to provide meaningful experiences and create connections that foster personal growth, strengthen relationships, and expose life-altering hope and trust. To be-*

come a transformative space for building relationships
among teams, between spouses, and with God.

By the time Truett died at age ninety-three in 2014,[119] the privately held company he had built had grown to more than 2,000 restaurants. It had approximately $6 billion in annual sales. His Christian witness lives on through Chick-fil-A restaurant employees and operators who daily carry his message of love and concern for each other and customers. It lives on through his Foundation's efforts to assist families and children to achieve successful and meaningful, Godly lives in service both to each other and to others. And it lives on through a legacy of kindness that cannot be measured.

---

[119] Trueet's wife Jeannette died at age 92 in 2015, the following year.

21

Drive-through, a Home for Orphans, and Wendy's

"Be kind to one another,
tenderhearted, forgiving one another,
as God in Christ forgave you."
— *Ephesians 4:32*

Dave Thomas

1932-2002

Christian entrepreneurs develop their careers from failing at one industry only to discover a better fit in another. Yet sometimes, they find the best career path for them out of early experiences in business and personal challenges. Rex David "Dave" Thomas was one of the later types. He was born in Atlantic City, New Jersey, to a young unmarried woman he never knew. Six weeks later, Rex and Auleva Thomas adopted him. When he was only five, Auleva died. Then, in the depth of the Great Depression, Rex had to move around the country, desperately chasing work. So, Dave spent some of his early childhood near Kalamazoo, Michigan, with his adoptive grandmother, Minnie Sinclair. His grandmother taught him the importance of service and treating others with respect and hospitality.

Dave received his first job at Regas Restaurant, Knoxville, Tennessee, at age twelve but lost the job shortly afterward in a dispute with his boss. This humiliating experience made Dave vow to never lose another job again. He continued to move with his father hunting for jobs. By age fifteen, in 1947, just two years after World War II ended, he found a part-time job in high school with the Clauss family who owned Hobby House Restaurant in Fort Wayne. When his dad had to move again, Dave decided to stay in Fort Wayne, drop out of high school, and work full time for the same employer. Later, Dave called this his biggest mistake. He did not earn his GED. And he did not graduate from high school until he was 61 years old.

At the beginning of the Korean War in 1950, at age eighteen, Dave volunteered for Army service before he was drafted. Because of that, he could choose the type of assignment. Naturally, he chose the Cook's and Baker's School at Fort Benning, Georgia, since nearly all of his teenage jobs had been restaurant work. Upon graduation, the Army sent him to Germany as a mess sergeant, responsible for feeding 2,000 soldiers. Three years later, after receiving an honorable discharge, Dave returned to Hobby House restaurant in Fort Wayne. In 1955 he married Lorraine.

Transforming KFC

While working at Hobby House, Dave met Colonel Harland Sanders,[120] the Kentucky Fried Chicken (KFC) franchise founder who was looking for established restaurant owners who might be interested in purchasing a KFC franchise. The KFC franchise network was still in its infancy. Harland sold the first franchise in 1952. Two years later, Harland visited Dave's employer's family. By this time, Dave had worked hard to advance up to head cook at Hobby House. Harland was persistent with the Clauss family until they finally relented about converting Hobby House into a KFC franchise. Before long, this family-owned many KFC franchises throughout the Midwest.

During this time, Dave developed a personal friendship with Harland. Since his employer became one of the largest owners of KFC franchises, Dave had plenty of opportunities to work directly with Harland on a variety of brand recognition and profitability projects. Dave suggested a reduction in the number of menu items and to center on a signature dish. Dave also suggested that Harland appear in his own company commercials to build a personal rapport with potential customers.

In the mid-1960s, the Clauss family sent Dave to help turn around four failing KFC restaurants they owned in Columbus, Ohio. Dave built sales substantially to the point where the Clauss family offered him partial ownership in the four restaurants to continue building their profits. By 1968, Dave had

---

[120] 1890–1980

caused sales in the four restaurants to soar. He was able to sell his share in the four restaurants to Harland for more than $1.5 million.

Later that year, Dave became part of an investor group started by a real estate developer who had built and leased several KFC properties. The investor group started a new fast-food franchise called Arthur Treacher's Fish and Chips.

Transforming Fast-Food

Dave cashed out of the new franchise in less than one year to start his own fast-food franchise. He named the new franchise after his eldest daughter, eight-year-old Melinda Lou—nicknamed "Wendy." Utilizing all the skills and experiences he had gained so far, Dave opened the first Wendy's Old Fashioned Hamburgers restaurant in November 1969.

In 1978 he started Sisters Chicken and Biscuits in honor of his other three daughters. These restaurants did not receive as much attention from Dave, and therefore their size never grew significantly. The companies he founded nonetheless provide insight into how important he felt family is.

By 1982, Dave resigned from managing daily operations. By that time, the company had more than 5,000 restaurants and became the third-largest fast-food hamburger chain globally. However, by 1985 other executives had made some strategic blunders, such as bad choices for a new breakfast menu, loss of brand awareness due to inadequate continuing funding for marketing and advertising, and similar issues. Dave let the new president keep his job, but returned to actively visiting the franchises to address these issues. During this time, he promoted his "mop bucket attitude"—Dave expected franchise owners to become personally involved with all aspects of their businesses and lead by example.

In 1989, Dave became the main spokesman in a series of television commercials. Dave was not a natural actor. To overcome his stiffness, an advertising agency helped portray him in a more self-deprecating, relaxed, folksy style, which proved very popular with potential and existing customers. This advertising campaign brought brand awareness and sales back to the company's all-time highs. Dave eventually appeared in more than 800 commercials—more than any other company founder in history up to that point. A survey found over 90 percent of Americans knew who Dave Thomas was.

Dave developed a high profile among the American public, received many awards, and even was appointed an honorary Kentucky colonel like his former boss. However, his impact was not limited to developing a chain of 6,000 restaurants to provide higher quality food at bargain prices and great service, including developing the concept of the drive-through window.

As an adult, Dave became a student at Coconut Creek High

School in Florida to earn his GED,[121] graduating only eight years before his death in hopes of inspiring young people to complete a good education. His work with Junior Achievement to encourage young entrepreneurs earned him induction into the organization's hall of fame in 1999. His traumatic early upbringing led him to give generously to church organizations and adoption agencies.

A Home for Children

Dave eventually formed the Dave Thomas Foundation for Adoption in 1992. His family and board created Dave Thomas Foundation for Adoption—Canada the year after his death in his honor. It is the only public, non-profit charity in the United States concentrating solely on providing loving permanent homes for all 110,000 foster children throughout North America. His foundation provides nearly 10,000 hours of training for other adoption agencies. It funds other adoption charities to hire specially-trained adoption recruiters whose sole mission is to find permanent, loving families for children at risk of aging out of the foster care system. The foundation also offers free resources to professionals as well as prospective and adoptive parents. Another major area of charitable effort Dave took personally was to become a strong education advocate.

He also founded the Dave Thomas Education Center at the Florida high school. There, he earned his GED to support and

---

[121] General Equivalency Diploma, which is considered the equivalent of a high school diploma.

encourage youth to complete their education and earn a solid start in life.

Dave did not fund or start a major church-related or missionary effort like some other Christian entrepreneurs. However, he said his faith in Jesus informed his charitable efforts to give back to those in need, starting with the two areas where his personal experiences informed him the most—high school education and showing love towards foster children like himself.

Dave lived out Biblical principles through his life and work—two key verses in particular. He demonstrated Ephesians 4:32. "Be kind to one another, tenderhearted, forgiving one another, as God in Christ forgave you." And he demonstrated Matthew 25:40. "And the King will answer them, 'Truly, I say to you, as you did it to one of the least of these my brothers, you did it to me." By showing love to others with the profits he earned, He did exactly as a Christian steward is called to do.

22

Developing Leadership and Vessels of Transformation

"Train champions for Christ."
— Jerry Falwell Senior

Jerry Falwell Sr.

1933-2007

Nobody's perfect. It's a simple statement, but true. Our next figure is a controversial one: Jerry Falwell Sr. Often, it's easiest to write about a visionary leader twenty, thirty years after their death. Scandals die down, the harsher aspects of their personalities and business dealings are less remembered, and the blessings of their legacies are more apparent to the next generation.

It is with this in mind that we will dive into the admittedly mixed legacy of Jerry Falwell Sr.—one of the most impactful leaders in the realm of Christian higher education. Despite his failings, through his innovations in televangelism, founding of Liberty University, and political action with the moral majority, God worked through Jerry Sr. to reach people with the gospel, educate the next generation, and speak out for political and religious freedom in the public arena. Business and politics have always been connected, but combining all three—charity, business, and politics—was the particular knack of Jerry Falwell Sr.

As we have seen in earlier biographies, entrepreneurs can build lasting charitable enterprises, which sometimes well outlast their for-profit cousins. A few even engage in entrepreneurial activity touching the political realm. Nearly all received business training—whether in the form of a degree or from the "school of hard knocks."

However, Jerry Sr. is known for having received his training in a totally different field—a divinity degree. God obviously gifted him with an insight into leadership skills, which he gladly trained others for. Yet, Jerry L. Falwell Sr. had a rough start in life in a town that had a bawdy reputation.

"Satan's Kingdom"

His grandfather was a staunch atheist who ran a moonshine still during Prohibition. His father was an agnostic bootlegger and alcoholic who shot his own brother in self-defense and had a reputation as a mean-spirited person. Despite being founded by a Quaker, John Lynch, the town of Lynchburg had developed a terrible reputation, since the late 1700s, because of the frequent public drunkenness, fights, prostitutes, and slave auctions. Evangelist Lorenzo Dow wrote in 1804:

> *Where I spoke in the open air in what I conceived to be the seat of Satan's Kingdom, Lynchburg was a deadly place for the worship of God.*

Growing up in such an environment, it is not surprising that Jerry Sr.'s initial exposure to the Christian faith came from listening to evangelical preachers on the radio. In the raucous town, business boomed. Jerry Sr.'s dad owned many local businesses and made lots of money. He was a gruff, demanding man who once killed, cooked, and served an employee's cat to him. Yet, at the same time, he was also a man who helped disadvantaged people in town and gave his family a comfortable lifestyle. Jerry Sr. learned hard work and generosity from his father's example.

At the age of 19, Jerry Sr. enrolled at Lynchburg College. It was there he would meet his future wife Macel while attending a local church service. In many ways, their upbringings were opposites. She was raised in a Christian home. He was raised in a rough, rebel home.

His mother and aunt prayed for his soul and his mother played Dr. Fuller's Old Fashioned Revival Hour on the radio every Sunday, and Jerry Sr. came to believe in Christ. Post conversion, instead of finishing a math major at Lynchburg College, his conversion experience led him to pursue the ministry to bring the Good News of Jesus to his hometown. To prepare, he attended Bible Baptist College in Springfield,

217

Missouri, then returned to Virginia at age 22. About this same time, a new pastor at Macel's church created a dispute with some church members. Unfortunately for Jerry Sr., the new pastor demanded that everyone who did not vote to call him leave immediately. Trouble was brewing.

The church founders who had voted against this pastor visited Jerry Sr., then in Richmond, to ask him to start a new church in Lynchburg. The other pastor was so vindictive that he got Jerry Sr. excommunicated by the Baptists Bible Fellowship International for not leaving Lynchburg and starting a "competing" congregation. But Jerry Sr. believed that God told him to stay and start Thomas Road Baptist Church.

Transforming Evangelism

Initially, Jerry Sr. knocked on 100 doors every day of the week except Sunday to build the new church. He developed a marketing guide to understanding all about every person in each of those homes throughout Lynchburg. With that detailed knowledge of the people, Jerry Sr. was able to build a large, rapidly growing congregation.

That same year, Jerry Sr. created the Old Time Gospel Hour on a local radio station. Jerry Sr. announced where he would be visiting in person each day. The show would go on to appear in another, increasingly popular media format: television. Jerry Sr. successfully negotiated a 30-minute television slot on a local ABC affiliate.[122]

The ABC time slot would go on to have more than 50 million regular viewers.

The TV program made him an instant celebrity. At the time, no other pastors were on TV, and few were on the radio. The success led to expansion. With no collateral to offer, he borrowed $5,000 for a building expansion and announced his goal to have 500 people in Sunday school the next week. A year before Falwell's television debut, church attendance was at 35 people. After the television program's broadcast, church attendance numbered some 864 congregants!

Thomas Road Baptist Church grew rapidly, as Jerry Sr. focused on sharing the life-changing Gospel message he had received with as many people as possible. Increasingly, he felt a strong desire to bring Jesus's message to youth and "train champions for Christ" who could transform and improve society in all walks of life. His first program beyond the church and both radio and TV programs was Elim Home for Alcoholics, established in 1959.

And his success in ministry was coupled with personal happiness. In 1958, Jerry Sr. finally won over Macel and convinced her parents to allow their marriage. The following year he began working on his major vision for ministry by launching

---

[122] The deal he worked out with the radio station cost him seven dollars per day, which was the equivalent of roughly half a day's typical wage at that time.

Lynchburg Christian Academy in 1967 for grades kindergarten through twelfth. The next four years were a financial challenge but an exhilarating period of growth for the school. Jerry Sr.'s ultimate vision was to provide an entire Christian education, from kindergarten through college, to equip Christian students for marketplace ministry in a wide variety of vocations, not just as pastors.

Racial Tensions

The year 1971 was a pivotal year for Jerry Sr. The 1970's saw the extension of the racial tensions and civil rights activism of the 1960's. It was in this period that Jerry Sr. saw firsthand how he was treated as a white American and how his African-American friend was treated. The contrast startled him. Jerry Sr. was also very honest about his history surrounding this issue, later admitting to a Harvard University audience that he had grown up as a racist during the Jim Crow era. However, a reckoning in his own beliefs about race came as he gradually realized the implications of his Christian faith.

When he preached in the Dominican Republic, a pastor there asked him not to mention race. "Here we work on our similarities, but you Americans point out the differences." His favorite shoeshine man in Lynchburg asked when he could join Thomas Road Baptist Church as a black man. These experiences caused Jerry Sr. to question the racial biases inherent in the Southern culture of the time, versus Jesus's message to care for everyone without any racial limitations. By studying the Bible's guidance on this issue, he changed his views about race to oppose racial discrimination as ungodly.

Interestingly, when he visited Duke University less than ten years after starting his own college, Jerry Sr. was challenged by an African-American student about how many black students attended his college. The Dean of the Chapel and a religious professor had to introduce him, but a student had invited him and Jerry Sr. insisted on giving a talk followed by a question and answer session, even though Duke University refused to pay his travel costs or a traditional honorarium.

There was much animosity expressed by Duke faculty and students leading up to this talk. Duke campus residents called Jerry Sr. a "closed-minded, racists, homophobic, self-righteous, incendiary" and anti-semitic in hopes of deterring Jerry Sr. from showing up. Instead, Jerry Sr. gave the talk with charm and grace. During the question period when the racism question arose, Jerry Sr. humbly and quickly admitted he wished his college could recruit more African-Americans. He discussed it with his friend Coretta Scott King, widow of Dr. Martin Luther King Jr. Quietly Jerry Sr. pointed out his college had a twelve percent minority enrollment at that time, versus Duke's six percent, despite Duke's endowment being fifty times larger. Duke's was a segregated university during half of the time of its existence. From that point, the Duke audience quietly and now respectfully listened to Jerry Sr.'s responses.

Transforming Christian Education

It was also in 1971 that Jerry Sr. founded Lynchburg Baptist College, later renamed Liberty Baptist College, then finally Liberty University (LU).[123] The initial startup was very hard.

The Old Time Gospel Hour had become a national program, generating many millions of dollars in donations. Some of those dollars were utilized to get the college started. Jerry Sr. rented space wherever he could make a low-cost deal around town—a vacant high school, a Ramada Inn, even a warehouse.

Liberty University started modestly, with only 154 students by offering a free study trip to Israel and asking donors across the nation to start with only one dollar per month in support of creating a world-class institution. Jerry Sr. believed "If it is Christian it should be better" so he negotiated a deal with the U.S. Gypsum Company, which owned Candler's Mountain just outside the city. Jerry Sr. asked for a 90-day option to buy it for $1.25 million, then worked hard to raise and borrow the funds, renaming the land Liberty Mountain.

By the second year, the faculty was up to 22 professors, mostly PhDs, and 420 students. At this point, Jerry Sr. purchased several hotels and an old hospital to house students. By 1976, enrollment rose to 1,871 students from 49 U.S. states and ten foreign nations. Their biggest draw was a high-quality education and Jerry Sr.'s determination to help them become

---

[123] Fondly known as LU by friends, students, and alumni of the Liberty University.

Champions for Christ.

Jerry Sr. was always on the move with the next initiative. He started Liberty Bible Institute in 1972, and Liberty Baptist Theological Seminary in 1973. Eventually, these institutions were absorbed into Liberty University. Jerry Sr. was the first Chancellor for each of these institutions, and he remained the active leader in all of his educational endeavors until his death.

During the mid-1970s, the university began offering an early form of distance education via taped lectures and printed course material. This was another rare innovation for an accredited higher education institution. The program is still in operation as of the publication of this book.

Faith has always been a prime generator for Liberty University. After a huge student prayer rally on Liberty Mountain in 1979, the school received $2.5 million and built its first 3,000 square foot multipurpose center. By the end of the fiscal year, an additional 21 buildings were under construction. Debt mounted to $82 million by 1981 for all of these buildings and initial losses: Tuition was kept low and affordable, plus Jerry Sr. frequently gave away tuition waivers to help needy students. Thankfully, the television ministry funded these early losses. In 1982 the university was admitted into NCAA (National Collegiate Athletic Association) Division II athletics, an exceptionally rapid achievement for a new, upstart university.

However, not all was well financially. In 1991, Liberty's debt had reached more than $ 100 million from non-stop building. That year a finance company backed out of a bond issue, causing all the short-term debt to default. The regional accreditation board pressured Jerry Sr. to address the 100 items needed to maintain the university's accreditation. Most of these items were minor, but the debt issue seemed insurmountable. Jerry Sr. prayed to God for time and guidance. And God responded: Liberty gradually worked down the debt to a manageable level by the later 1990s.

By 1996, the university had 5,500 students on a $200 million 3,000 acre campus. Around this time, President Bush and other national leaders began coming to LU to speak. Shortly after this period, Jerry Sr. explored the new Internet phenomena and its more economic ability to bring affordable courses and degree programs to students worldwide. This idea was explosive. LU became the second-largest online higher education institution in the world and number one among non-profit educational institutions with more than 100,000 students.

Vessels of Transformation

Liberty University was clearly Jerry Sr.'s greatest entrepreneurial achievement. However, he also created other organizations, some of which were highly controversial. Perhaps the organization creating the greatest resistance from more leftist critics was Moral Majority, Inc. Jerry Sr. originally believed that ministers should stay away from politics, especially political and societal change. He eventually realized this position was not Biblical, as other Christian entrepreneurs before him had discerned. In response to the anti-life Supreme Court decision to overturn every abortion law throughout the nation base on no precedent, Jerry Sr. agonized over whether Christians could "render unto Caesar" by becoming involved in political issues when the government failed in its responsibilities.

Calling together a group of national advisors in 1979, he formed the Moral Majority to express a Christian witness in the political arena and encourage Christians to vote for their values without intimidation. In only two years, the organization mobilized over 100,000 religious leaders to register 7 million voters, crediting them with making a significant contribution to electing Ronald Reagan as president of the United States and defeating 11 Democrat Senators. The organization was a strong force supporting candidates expressing Christian values and principles for ten years, from 1979-1989.

This was not the only social justice project Jerry Sr. started. In 1982 he formed Liberty Godparent Home for Unwed Mothers. In 1985 he built Liberty Broadcasting Network, for which he remained president until his death. In his determination to transform society towards Christianity, Jerry recognized that the everyday people were the most important vessel of such transformation. He frequently found time to chat with students, give speeches around the world, and meet with presidents and prime ministers—from the U.S. to Egypt—to break bread and provide a Christian perspective. In his spare time, he led missionary and humanitarian efforts in nations around the world, often giving Liberty students an opportunity to participate.

As with other entrepreneurs, there were several major challenges along the road to success. A huge challenge came in the form of a Securities and Exchange Commission (SEC) investigation. In 1973, the SEC investigated Thomas Road Baptist Church for issuing bonds to fund Liberty University when there were questions about the solvency and disclosure of the full financial situation. By that time, Thomas Road had grown to 13,000 members, and the TV program was seen on over 300 stations across America. Jerry Sr. had started yet another initiative—Elim. Elim was a home for men with alcohol and drug addictions, which was a cash drain, as was the college. Around this time, a fellow pastor visited Jerry Sr. to teach him the value of prayer and waiting on God to refresh himself. The SEC eventually concluded there was no misstatement.

Another big challenge occurred from Jerry Sr. trying to help another ministry. A few years before, Jim and Tammy Bakker had started a large television ministry. By 1986, the Bakkers had committed bankruptcy fraud. In the resulting aftermath, they asked Jerry Sr. to take over the board of PTL Ministries. Upon accepting control of PTL Ministries, Jerry Sr. quickly found the Bakkers were continuing to lie about the abuse of donations and were misleading about further the sexual and financial sins which bankrupted their ministry. Needless to say, Jerry Sr. was not pleased.

In response, Jerry Sr. and the entire board of PTL Ministries resigned. It was clear the Bakkers were unrepentant and were, in fact, trying to continue their fraudulent behavior and transfer the consequence to Jerry Sr. and the other board members. Jerry Sr. publicly called them on this, resulting in the Bakkers suing Jerry Sr. for defamation. Jerry Sr. was very upset, not only about being personally lied to and used, but especially for the Bakkers giving all TV evangelists a damaged reputation with the general public. Despite the lawsuit and his resignation, Jerry Sr. attempted to save donors from additional abuse. He successfully kept the Bakkers from regaining control of PTL Ministries.

However, reporters eager for headline-making scandals tried to damage Jerry Sr. and other ministries' reputations. Donations to all of Jerry Sr.'s ministry efforts dropped, although student attendance continued to grow. Gradually, Jerry Sr. helped restore the good reputation for LU and other legitimate ministries hurt by the Bakker scandal's bad publicity. For a while, reporters would jokingly ask him if he had done anything controversial lately so they could boost their shows' ratings.

Amongst all this, Jerry Sr. found time to publish 21 books between 1971 and 2006. That's an average of one book every two years! Considering all the many organizations Jerry Sr. started, his busy travel schedule, frequent chats with students, ministerial duties, and family obligations, it is amazing Jerry Sr. could write so many books!

The early 2000s saw Jerry Sr. seeing many of his entrepreneurial visions come to pass. David Green, the owner of Hobby Lobby, donated the $10,550,000 needed to buy LU's second-largest building in 2003. The university was living up to its mission to train champions for Christ and change the world for Jesus. By the time Jerry Sr. passed away, Liberty

University had become the second-largest online education provider in the world, the largest university of any kind in Virginia, and the largest Christian university in the entire world. Jerry Sr. had one more gift for his higher education ministry.

Jerry Sr. had a great deal of foresight about the short-term finance of the University. He had taken out tens of millions of dollars in life insurance policies. Upon his death, these policies paid off the remaining debt for the university. This enabled the university to finally reach a very healthy financial state with multi-billion dollar endowments, massive new building projects, expansion of educational ministry into new fields, including schools of law and medicine, Division I sports status, and other achievements that older universities have taken a century or two to reach. These resources have allowed Liberty University to truly achieve Jerry Sr.'s vision of creating champions for Christ in all major fields of study.

23

Hospitality, Family, and Marvel Cave

"We best serve the Lord by bringing families together."
— The Herschend Brothers

Jack & Pete Herschend

1928 & 1930 - Current

Christian entrepreneurs pour many years of hard work and intensive commitment into achieving their dreams. But our next set of entrepreneurs succeeded by having fun and bringing more fun to many others. Jack and Pete Herschend enjoyed vacationing in Missouri's Ozark Mountains. They visited Branson in 1946. Since they enjoyed it so much, their parents leased a cave in the area—Marvel Cave. They planned to develop it as a tourist site while continuing to sell vacuum cleaners to support the family. Branson was physically about 550 miles from Chicago. Culturally, it was a world apart.

The boys thoroughly enjoyed exploring the cave. In the immense caverns of the wet limestone cave, they found very old fossils that the boys convinced the Natural History Museum of New York to carbon-date for them. They also discovered an underground lake with blind, translucent salamanders.

Jack fell in love with a local girl, Sherry, whom he married in the cave in 1954 at age twenty-six. In the beginning, the cave was lit only by candles. However, the family gradually added electricity and other amenities to make the cave an increasingly engaging tourist attraction. As the family expanded their entertainment options around the cave, they found that their cave lease from the Lynch sisters did not cover twenty parcels of land around the cave, where a former town had existed in the late 1800s, and which they needed for additional customer parking. The brothers bought out the Lynch sisters plus these additional properties, investing all of their savings to buy these parcels plus bring water and electricity to the cave. They then planned to rebuild the former town, a former stagecoach trail stop, and a small mining operation as an 1880s Old West-style town named Silver Dollar City.

Silver Dollar City

The brothers stretched their finances to borrow $18,000 and tried to rebuild the town themselves in an attempt to keep costs low while building an authentic town, not simply storefronts. They could not complete the job themselves, so they hired Russ Pearson from Oklahoma City, who said they were all wrong in their approach. He rebuilt the town into the current Silver Dollar City amusement park. This experience also helped teach the brothers to seek wise advisors.

The new Silver Dollar City opened in 1960. The brothers picked that name because they initially gave silver dollars as change to park visitors. Visitors used the silver dollars to buy gas and other items on their way home, causing many people to ask where they received the silver dollars. Vacationers described the park and their adventures. This word-of-mouth exposure proved to be a tremendous marketing campaign at a low price. The small staff of only seventeen (including the brothers and Jack's wife) dressed in 1880s costumes and performed street theater, including funny presentations of the Hatfields and McCoys. The first year of Silver Dollar City's operation generated over 125,000 visitors—quadrupling the number of cave visitors.

In 1963 the brothers invited native artisans to demonstrate nineteen varieties of crafts such as woodcarving, tie hacking, blacksmithing, candle-making, etc. In subsequent years they added other crafts such as glass blowing, silversmith, potter, etc. The craft demonstrations were a hit from the very first year, bringing more than a half-million visitors to the theme park that first year. The park rapidly became Missouri's top tourist attraction.

In 1966 Pete married JoDee at their Silver Dollar City theme park. Just a few years later, in 1969, the cast and crew of the hit television series Beverly Hillbillies filmed five episodes at Silver Dollar City. This marketing exposure drew a huge increase in park visitors, providing enough cash flow to add additional entertainment, such as stagecoach rides, a steam train, theater, and much more.

By 1998 the park was attracting more than 2,000,000 visitors annually, expanding into more crafts demonstrated by one hundred craftsmen over an area now encompassing approximately one hundred acres. The company continued to thrive, adding many additional wholesome entertainment properties, such as:

- Dollywood, previously Silver Dollar City in Tennessee—Pigeon Forge, Tennessee
- Wild Adventures—Valdosta, Georgia
- White Water Water Park—Branson, Missouri
- Dollywood's Splash Country—Pigeon Forge, Tennessee
- Adventure Aquarium—Camden, New Jersey
- Newport Aquarium[124]—Newport, Kentucky
- Stone Mountain—company took over management of this state park and added a theme park
- Talking Rocks Caverns—Branson West, Missouri
- Pirates Voyage—Myrtle Beach, South Carolina
- Dolly Parton's Stampede Dinner Show, Showboat Branson Belle, Dolly Parton's Smoky Mountain Adventures, and Dollywood's DreamMore ResortEnd—all a part of Dollywood

Over the years, the brothers reorganized under an umbrella company called Herschend Enterprises, which owns three major subsidiaries:

---

[124] Opened in 1999 along with the charitable Wave Foundation.

- Herschend Family Entertainment[125]
- Harlem Globetrotters[126]
- Herschend Studios[127]

In total, the brothers own twenty-six entertainment properties in twelve states. Many top country and pop music performers have entertained at their Grand Palace theater in Branson.

All this commercial success has provided wholesome family entertainment for seventy-one million guests since 1960, contributing over $100 million to the Missouri state economy in addition to boosting other states' economies and providing jobs to more than 35,000 people over the years. While the brothers are worth an estimated $150 million each, that is not the major benefit for them. Golden Ticket (an entertainment industry association) in 2009 voted Silver Dollar City as the friendliest park in the entire theme park industry. Ernst & Young, the top tier worldwide accounting and consulting firm in 2005 named them Entrepreneurs of the Year in the Central Midwest. Yet the brothers have given back much more than they received.

They each have been very active, giving back their time and money to improve the communities where they operate. For example, Jack began a reforestation program recognized by the National Arbor Day Foundation. He serves on the boards

---

[125] Owns all the properties, including lodges. Formed 1950.

[126] Acquired in 2013.

[127] Started in 2015.

of several organizations, including Lives Under Construction Boys Ranch, Kids Across America, and the National Institute of Marriage.

His brother Pete serves as board chairman of Upper White River Basin Foundation, and he is on the board of Camp Barnabas. Pete is the longest-serving member of the Missouri State Board of Education.[128] He has served on the boards of Missouri Attractions Association and Travel Industry Association of America and International Association of Amusement Parks & Attractions, and Ozark Marketing Council. Pete was named Education Supporter of the Year in 2012 by the Missouri Chamber of Commerce for his strong commitment to improving youth's educational opportunities. They partnered with Wave Foundation in conjunction with their Kentucky aquarium. This foundation's mission is to "excite, engage and educate our community about the wonders of aquatic life and the importance of conservation."

Jack and Pete have provided a great example of the leadership concept referred to as Quadruple Bottom Line Goals: every organization must have financial goals in order to assure its sustainability. However, most companies stop with just that category of goal.

Other businesses and nearly all "non-profit" organizations develop a second set of goals: social enhancements or environmental concerns. A small but growing number of companies will have social and environmental goals and the basic finan-

---

[128] Since 1991.

cial set of goals.

But with very rare exceptions, only Christian entrepreneurs add a fuller fourth dimension—spiritual goals. An example of Herschend environmental goals is the Wave Foundation support mentioned earlier and their careful planning at each park to keep in mind how to bring the colorful history of each geographic region to life so customers can easily understand and enjoy the experience and context while nurturing the environment. An example of social efforts is reflected in the goal of their Harlem Globetrotters company. The team, its media productions, and the entire merchandising line are all designed with the goal of "continuing the brand's legacy of deep social involvement in local communities." This is especially important for giving inner-city kids role models and inspirational examples of how to succeed in life.

But there is a much deeper and more lasting commitment to helping their communities through that fourth dimension of spiritual help. The Herschend companies endeavor to live their mission statement intentionally each day:

> *Creating memories worth repeating, we bring families closer together.*

Even this mission statement only summarizes the full scope. The brothers grew up in a home that was not really Christian. Their parents took them to Sunday school but did not attend church themselves and were not really Christians. Christianity was simply not a factor growing up. Both wives were Christians and led the brothers to faith. This has brought them a realization that just as Jesus is Lord over all of life's activities, they want to bring Biblical understanding into their business, family, and charitable efforts. As Jack and Pete explained it a few years ago in an interview, their core personal and business values start with Jesus. They want their witness to be "tasteful" by example and a gentle explanation of how Jesus can transform lives.

Bringing Families Together

Their company vision statement reads, "We best serve the Lord by bringing families together." The company's emphasis is wholesome entertainment that helps bring families together to enjoy time with each other. Another value is honoring their employees and treating them like family. They implement this value by listening and making sure each employee feels valued. When a decision affects them, employees get an opportunity to speak into it. The corporate culture and theme park atmosphere they have very intentionally cultivated displays their faith in action.

"We're about honoring God, honoring Christ as our Savior, outside of the church. We are in the entertainment business; we are not in the business of the church. But if we do it right, then hopefully thousands of families will sense that unique heart and soul."

"That heart and soul includes the freedom of our men and women to talk about Christ when it's appropriate. It is the freedom to have church services at the park. Those are all part of the core values. And if you read our mission statement, it says that we create memories worth repeating. But one statement says it all, that we do what we do in a manner consistent with Christian values. Everything. You have to do it that way. You can't just say, 'We do that a lot.' It has to be the heart and soul."

As part of their effort to share their Christian faith with customers, the brothers started the practice of church services in the Silver Dollar City Wilderness Church building from their very early days every Sunday and continue that tradition today. Throughout the week, employees sing Christian hymns and songs in the Wilderness Church.

After Jack and Pete retired, they hired Joel Manby, a Christian, to be their company CEO. Joel was on the TV show Undercover Boss. CBS left in the Christian values mentioned—perhaps because they are such an integral part of what makes the company so special. This surprised the brothers.

Jack and Pete also started a "Share It Forward" fund for employees who have personal needs. Their CEO started another employee fund specifically to assist single mothers and single dads living below the poverty line as a result of working "undercover" next to some lower-income employees and hearing about their struggles. These efforts show a Christlike family concern for employees and their families well beyond what most companies are willing to do today.

Lead with Love

Sharing God's Word extends beyond all of these efforts into the rest of the business community, including competitors. Herschend Enterprises publishes on its website a *Lead with Love Foundational Principles*:

- Patient—Have self control in difficult situations
- Kind—Show encouragement and enthusiasm
- Humble—Enable and celebrate the success of others
- Respectful—Treat each other with dignity, honor, and courtesy
- Trusting—Place confidence in others
- Unselfish—Think of yourself less
- Forgiving—Release the grip of the grudge
- Truthful—Define reality corporately and individually
- Dedicated—Stick to your values in all circumstances

The company developed a *Lead with Love* curriculum and consulted with other like-minded companies and entrepreneurs interested in bringing these principles into their businesses. The Herschend brothers commit staff and resources to promote and support this effort. They also hold an annual *Lead with Love Conference* since 1950 as a two-day event "to educate and empower corporate leaders to create a *Lead with Love* culture that can engage employees and create value for all stakeholders."

In conjunction with this conference and personalized company consulting, the company also offers a book entitled *Herschend Family Values: Creating Memories Worth Repeating.* This book includes some of their personal experiences plus stories from other Christian entrepreneurs. Some stories are funny, many are inspiring, and some are heartbreaking stories that all "help us imagine new ways to bring families closer together."

In one interview, Jack and Pete were asked what advice they would suggest to anyone considering starting a business. Their advice to new Christian entrepreneurs is to surround yourself with the right people. The Bible talks about being equally yoked concerning marriage partners, but this also makes sense in a business. "It's really important to have Christians with you as you get started" but later hire some non-believers "because that is an opportunity to witness."

24

Stewardship, Wisdom, and Strategic Air Command

"How we use our money
is the clearest outside indicator
of what we really believe"
— Larry Burkett

Larry Burkett

1939-2003

Can a Christian entrepreneur make a major impact upon society by advising others? The next entrepreneur did just that. Larry Burkett took the long route to become a Christian entrepreneur and advisor to other Christians, both to entrepreneurs and wage earners. Larry was the fifth of eight children born into a poor family in Florida during the Great Depression. His family, who were not Christians, lacked family unity. This was a frequent source of stress as he grew up.

Strategic Air Command

Upon graduating high school in Winter Garden, Florida, Larry joined the Air Force and served for a time in the Strategic Air Command. While in the Air Force, Larry met his wife Judy, and they were married in 1958. Upon release from the Air Force, he worked as a civilian employee at Cape Canaveral Space Center. He was placed in charge of several experimental test facilities involved in the Mercury, Gemini, and Apollo programs. While working at the Space Center, Larry earned a Bachelor of Finance degree and then a Master of Economics degree through an Air Force scholarship and passed the professional licensing exam to become a Certified Public Accountant (CPA).

In 1970, at the age of thirty-one, he left the Space Center to become Vice President and a co-founder of a firm, which manufactured electronic test equipment, with a friend, near Gainsville, Georgia. 1970 was an eventful and stressful year for Larry in more ways than one. The same year he took on the challenge of launching a new corporation, his wife became a Christian. Judy tried to talk with Larry about the Bible and how Jesus had brought such joy to her life, but Larry was annoyed and wanted his wife back. Larry resisted in every way he could think of but eventually agreed to attend a weekly Bible class—but not worship services. Larry argued strongly against each point and fact every chance he got in that Bible class. At that time, Larry's beliefs or worldview could best be described as agnostic. He believed there probably was some sort of god, but he had no personal connection.

The pastor who attempted to lead that Bible study eventually

241

grew weary of Larry's constant complaining and opposition. Pointing out that Larry was too disruptive and argumentative to allow anyone else to learn anything from the Bible study, the pastor challenged Larry to read the Bible for himself, by himself, without seeking to design attacks attempting to destroy his wife's faith—just absorb the information. The pastor said that after Larry had read the entire Bible, he would be willing to meet answer any objections. If Larry still had any doubts after reading the Bible himself, then the Bible was clearly not for him. The pastor promised that, if that was the case, he and the other members of the church would no longer encourage him to read the Bible or attend any church functions.

Larry explored God's message on his own for two years. While he was reading he tried to keep an objective and open mind to critically analyze. At the age of thirty-two, after reading and critiquing the whole Bible alone, Larry found so much evidence that he accepted Jesus as his Savior. After this conversion experience, Larry began attending the Bible study and church worship services. At first, the pastor was wary. He had become so frustrated and angry at Larry's previous aggressive behavior that the pastor had stormed out of Larry's house in frustration. However, after Larry accepted Christ's love, the pastor noticed continual substantial changes in Larry's behavior and attitude. Within a year, the man who was discharged for being too disruptive to attend a Bible study was asked to lead one of his own to teach the deep insights Larry was gaining from his solitary research.

Transforming Christian Finances

One of the topics in the Bible which caught Larry's attention was money. Larry identified over 1,000 passages about money. It took him several years to categorize them all. Then he began to work on the first of seventy books on Biblical stewardship principles he discovered from the Bible. Over the next few years, Larry became known as such a Biblical money expert that Dallas Theological Seminary invited him to teach their professors about Biblical money principles. Bill Bright of Campus Crusade for Christ met Larry and asked him to sell his young entrepreneurial electronics company ownership interest to join Campus Crusade for one year. This one-year commitment became two and a half years, as Larry continued to grow in Biblical understanding and a desire to share that understanding to help people in their daily lives. During this time working for Bill Bright, Larry published his first book on Christian principles of personal financial management.

In 1976, Larry felt called to focus on sharing specifically what the Bible had to say concerning personal money management. He noticed so many people were struggling financially during the "stagflation"—simultaneous extremely high inflation combined with terrible economic stagnation and high job losses—due to the Ford and Carter administrations' mismanagement of the United States economy. So in 1976, Larry launched his own non-profit financial counseling firm called Christian Financial Concepts. This was the first firm to provide financial advice based upon a Christian perspective, and one of the very few was a non-profit organization. Some of the Biblical concepts were ridiculed by secular advisors as impractical or not in the client's best interests. Still, Larry persisted, helping many people to develop a secure financial future for their families while also learning how to return some of this abundance to God in support of the Biblical calling to share with the less fortunate and help others.

Over the following decade, the firm prospered. The staff expanded to more than one hundred employees providing Christian financial advice to individuals and small businesses throughout all of America and many other nations world-wide. His seventy books have sold more than eleven million copies and have reached the national bestsellers list several times. During this period, Larry developed three radio programs—Money Matters, How to Manage Your Money, and MoneyWatch—plus a series of short features titled "A Money Minute." These popular radio programs expanded into over 1,100 radio stations worldwide in various languages. In addition to all this, his firm pumped out countless money management courses and workbooks for churches, home study groups, and families to utilize for their members' or their own personal benefit.

Somewhere in between all the worldwide speaking engage-ments, managing a growing organization, broadcasting radio shows, and more, Larry also published four fiction novels designed to illustrate how financial troubles can hurt people without warning. The novels also showed how to become aware of these trends early and what actions would best mitigate potential financial troubles. These novels were more about the macro view of societal ignorance of Biblical economic principles, the potential harm this turning away from healthy economic management can cause, and what individuals can do to reduce the pain and help others through difficult times. In May 1996, Southwest Baptist University conferred an honorary doctorate in economics for the tremendous clarification Larry had provided to so many people about Biblical money management principles.

Larry's early decision to undertake his own study of money in the Bible led to a worldwide movement on godly stewardship. In 2000 he changed the name of his firm to Crown Financial Ministries.[129] Through his entrepreneurial firm, Larry has trained over two million people through small group studies to better manage their own money in a way that is more consistent with Biblical principles. He wrote books not only for adults to use in understanding godly money concepts but also published for teens and fellow business owners. One book in particular, *Business by the Book*, caused other Christian business owners to seek more information on how to engage in marketplace ministry efforts.

Joining with other Atlanta-area Christian business owners, Larry was a co-founder of Christian Business Fellowship in 1977. He became very active in 1980, teaching and advising Christian business owners how to conduct business according to biblical principles and to carry out the Great Commission through their companies. By 1989 the organization had changed its name to Fellowship of Companies for Christ International (FCCI) to reflect its rapidly expanding scope.

---

[129] The organization's website is www.crown.org.

Partnering in Transformation

During the exciting development of FCCI and Crown Financial
Ministries, one of the people Larry hired was Ron Blue, who is
also a Christian CPA. Ron's professional career started at one of
the major CPA firms, working out of offices in several different
states. In 1970 Ron founded a CPA firm in Indianapolis, which
grew into one of the fifty largest accounting firms in America.
Leaving that firm in 1977, he became a vice president at
Leadership Dynamics International for a brief time. This
company provides executive coaching services to improve
leaders and companies' effectiveness and profitability.

While there, Ron became involved in developing and teaching Bible-based seminars around America and Africa as a
contractor with Larry's firm. As Ron's interest in Christian
money management grew, he left Leadership Dynamics to
launch yet another firm called Ronald Blue Trust. This firm
has grown to provide financial advice to families from the
very poor and middle class to wealthy families needing special
services. Ron's goal is similar to Larry's objective—to show
Christians how to manage and spend their finances in a God-
pleasing manner. The firm grew to manage over $2 billion in
assets for over 5,000 clients worldwide as an independent fee-
only firm with 175 staff in fourteen regional offices around the
United States. Ron sold the firm to Thrivent Trust Company[130]
in 2003 to pursue his goal of engaging in Great Commission
work through Kingdom Advisors, training Christian financial

---

[130] It started as a mutual aid society for Lutherans which now is a non-
denominational non-profit money management firm.

advisors.

Larry and Ron wrote a few books together and their careers intertwined: Larry pioneered a movement, while Ron carries on a similar vision today. Larry's core work branched off into Ron's money management services and FCCI's business owner ministry support. Larry's Crown Ministries also offers resources to business owners.

Larry wanted to bring financial freedom and an understanding of how to apply that freedom to accomplish God's calling in each person's life to many individuals. While building his financial education firm, Larry became concerned about the growing hostility against Christians expressing their constitutional right to share their faith with other people. Larry joined with a group of Christian leaders to form an organization called Alliance Defending Freedom to protect and defend Christian freedom. This organization consists of a network of attorneys litigating to protect Christian Americans' First Amendment rights, live out their faith in the marketplace and all areas of their daily lives.

Nothing to Fear

His last several years leading up to his death were not easy for Larry. His health declined, and he suffered through increasing challenges in his fight against cancer. During those last few years, he founded the Larry Burkett Cancer Research Foundation to help other cancer patients live longer and more productive lives, even though his cancer had been diagnosed as terminal. His last two books provide a testament to Larry's trust in Jesus. One of the books was entitled *Nothing to Fear*, describing his experiences with cancer. The other book, co-authored with Ron Blue and Jeremy White, was named *The Burkett & Blue Definitive Guide to Securing Wealth to Last*. As you may have guessed, the "last" part not only discusses funding all of retirement, it offers guidance on how to provide a truly lasting legacy in heaven, where money and other fleeting material assets are irrelevant. Larry believed that this was the legacy that mattered most. And this was the kind of legacy he left behind.

25

Mark Up, Margin, and Might at Hobby Lobby

*"Whatever your hand finds to do,
do it with your might..."*
— *Ecclesiastes 9:10*

David Green

1941-current

A Christian entrepreneur's business need not overtly proclaim Jesus for the business owner to be a strong witness in the community. If the business is run according to biblical principles, the world will notice—including the court system. Like other business heroes of the faith profiled in this book, David has not been afraid to face societal giants to proclaim the truth of God's Word consistently.

The Crucial Business Idea

David Green was born into a financially struggling family of preachers at the tail end of the Great Depression and the very cusp of America entering World War II. Unfortunately, he was not a good student at the small Altus, Oklahoma high school he attended. Altus, which is nearly halfway between Oklahoma City and Amarillo, Texas, was almost 200 miles from any real opportunities for good employment—the proverbial "middle of nowhere."

David signed up for a "work-study" school program to learn a trade to support himself. He first worked at McClellan's, a small local retail store. David's meager income helped supplement his dad's meager pastoral pay. Sometimes his dad was paid in farm crops rather than money by the poor congregates. From the beginning of this work-study program, young David worked at organizing store operations to be more efficient. He learned to pay close attention to detail from Mr. Tyler, the owner of McClellan's. Tyler also taught David the retail concept of mark up and margin, which became the crucial business idea propelling David's later success.

David met his future wife, Barbara, at McClellan's: He was a stock boy and she was a clerk. After high school, David enlisted in the Air Force, even though both World War II and the Korean War were over. When he left the Air Force at nineteen, they were married. The following year, he began working for a retail chain called TG&Y—a "five and dime" type of larger store chain which started in rural areas during the Depression. During the years he worked for TG&Y, David advanced from clerk to store manager. Around this time, David and Barbara were blessed with the birth of their three children.

In 1970, while still working at TG&Y, David and a friend from TG&Y borrowed $600 from a bank to start a picture frame making business. David, his partner, and his wife, along with their two young sons (their daughter was still too young to help out at that time), all made picture frames in their garage at night and on the weekends. David and his partner convinced a traveling salesman to solicit orders while selling other items during his wanderings. The salesman successfully obtained numerous orders from other retail stores throughout the Southwestern United States.

Within two years, the business—named Greco Products—boomed. With their newfound profits, David and his wife bought out the partner and rented a 300 square foot store in northwestern Oklahoma City where they had been transferred to by TG&Y. In 1975, David left his job at TG&Y and took a leap of faith to open a second store location with a huge 6,000 square feet of space. By this time, he had renamed the business Hobby Lobby.

Hobby Lobby

This big risk was not without challenges. David believes risk-taking is an essential requirement to build a business, but he also believes that the risk must be limited to what circumstances permit. He recognizes that taking risks is also a step out in faith. It is trusting in God. With this in mind, he prayed over every major business decision and continued to make substantial donations to spread the Gospel message further, even when cash flows would periodically dip. For example, one way David limited risk was by building the shelves in the first few Hobby Lobby stores out of 2 x 4 lumber and 1 x 12 boards with his own hands.

Early on, store cash flow dropped for a while, so the bank holding his note began foreclosure proceedings on his defaulted obligation. In an effort to save the store, David pursued many different banks until he found one he could convince to provide a line of credit, thereby preventing the foreclosure. In a rare burst of pride, David framed and hung the foreclosure notice on his lobby wall, but later felt God was teaching him humility through this business challenge, so he removed the notice. The next week, David heard the president of his old bank who had sought to close his business had suffered a personal tragedy. The bank president's wife died in a car accident. Through this, David had the opportunity to provide Chrisitan witness and comfort to the bank president. This helped David understand God's perspective that his business dealings occur to give God the glory and share the Bible message of hope in very personal settings, not to gloat over temporary commercial victories.

Four Fundamentals for Retail Success

David developed four fundamental retailing success principles which are taught to every employee:

- Run your business in harmony with God's laws. That is

ethics.

- Focus on people more than money: Always seek the customer's perspective, and get the right people in the right positions.
- Be a merchant: Concentrate on buying and selling, while minimizing everything else.
- Install the right systems to support the first three goals.

The foundational concept from which David derived these principles is expressed in Ecclesiastes 9:10: "Whatever your hand finds to do, do it with your might..." Be the best competitor you can while encouraging employees to be servants, even in a self-serve store. Warehouse and corporate office staff are told they have jobs to make things convenient for store managers, not the reverse. Hobby Lobby sends buyers worldwide and turns over 50,000 new items annually, refreshing the shopping experience for their target market of women who want to improve their homes.

This focus on Biblical concepts for business has created some unique corporate policies. Contrary to nearly all modern retail companies, Hobby Lobby maintains minimal computerized processes. For example, rather than encouraging barcodes on products, it is prohibited. The purpose is to ensure employees know every product and respond to customers quicker. He emphasized the idea of keeping it simple. With very few exceptions, every store is stocked the same, and managers spend minimal time on paperwork to maximize time with customers and employees.

David freely writes about the management metrics he uses.

Store managers are the key employees to running a successful retail operation. He first applies five reviews:

1. Shopping atmosphere
2. Orderliness
3. Spaciousness
4. Helpfulness
5. Ambiance

Managers are also evaluated on quick product turnover with steep discounts encouraged on items that do not sell, regardless of the loss.

Guarding the Bottom Line

He uses three methods to guard the bottom line.

1. Cost control on products requires only direct purchase from manufacturers without go-betweens. Bulk purchases are stored in the company's large Oklahoma City warehouse. Everything is recycled (boxes, scraps, shipping wrapping, etc.), and they sometimes make new products from these materials in-house, such as frames and candles.
2. Overhead costs are limited to a maximum of 11 percent of each store's gross sales for local wages, rent, and all other expenses, which the local store manager can personally control. Store locations are not always in the prime locations to keep costs low. While David supplies

guidelines on liability insurance, cleaning, and other expenses, the local manager has total discretion subject to the 11 percent overall cap. Store managers receive bonuses for below-average costs, and the averages for all stores nationwide are publicized among all managers.

3. Space in the three million square foot warehouse and general corporate overhead are measured by the cost of product shipped per employee hour reported each week. One tractor-trailer per store is equipped with extra-sized fuel tanks. All fuel is bulk purchased in Oklahoma City to obtain the lowest wholesale fuel costs. All drivers are required to backhaul loads for other companies when returning to the warehouse to offset the cost of trucking even further. The corporate headquarters and store managers advertise category sales rather than individual products. Basic restocking is based on three statistics: sales volume per store, percent of entire chain's sales represented per store, and how many of a particular item sold across the entire chain each month.

As you can see, these measurements provide strong account-ability, greater flexibility, and worthwhile incentives for managers.

Priorities

The corporate priorities—in order of importance—as told to the manager, headquarters staff, and executives, are as follows:

1. Serving God
2. Serving people
3. Being a merchant
4. Systems (which exist only to make the first three priorities possible)

David and his son hold minimal monthly meetings and conduct all of them on the same day. First officers and buyers provide an overview, then thirty-six buyers have a detailed discussion of customer demands and product available products. The third meeting is with merchandising managers, followed by an officers luncheon to discuss company-wide concerns. Finally, the Board of Directors reviews policy. David set an example of listening and adjusting quickly, letting employees make mistakes without much consequence as long as their values align with corporate policies. The Green family and their executives allow great freedom at the store level to managers regarding how to operate each store. Managers and employees bear the risk of losing bonuses if they make bad decisions. They also earn bonuses for good decisions—thus providing the necessary personal accountability alongside the freedom to make decisions at low levels in the company.

Part of the ethical policy includes no gifts from vendors ever, no matter how small. This applies to everyone, not just buyers. As David says to employees, "character counts." He wants all employees to be pro-customer, not swayed by any incentives from those vendors trying to get Hobby Lobby to purchase their goods, even though this policy runs contrary to industry norms. David came to recognize that God understands business and the need for profits, but He cares more for our hearts. Eventually, this caused the emphasis of David's goals to shift from success to significance. As he explains it, the measure of a person's life is not how many assets he or she accumulates but how we align ourselves with God's purposes so we can impact eternity.

This attitude of focusing on kingdom-oriented goals rather than earthly financial goals has expanded the original company into twelve companies worldwide. Hobby Lobby now has more than 300 stores nationwide with $1.4 billion in annual sales. David's estimated net worth is approximately $5 billion.

In the last decade, he turned over daily management to one of his sons, but David remains chairman of eight of the affiliated companies. Starting from the initial $600 bank loan, David has avoided requests to take the company public. He watched the impact upon fellow Christian entrepreneurs who offered stock to the public. For example, Sam Walton was pressured to give up Bible-based principles and donations to support ministry from non-believing stockholders who could not comprehend the bigger issues. With the Green family maintaining ownership, they have been able to generously support many ministry efforts and cannot be inhibited from running Hobby Lobby as a Christian marketplace ministry.

Ministry in Business and Beyond

Two recent examples—besides the unique operating culture of the company itself—highlight this ministry approach. For many years, David and his sons have purchased Bible artifacts around the world. They donated a collection estimated to be worth over $180 million, additional funds, and leadership to create the Museum of the Bible, which opened in Washington, DC, in 2017. The aim of the 400,000 square foot technology-oriented museum is to continue researching the impact of the Bible in history and society. It also invites people from all walks of life to discover the message of the Bible and how it has transformed humankind.

Another example of marketplace ministry impact is the highly heralded Supreme Court lawsuit in 2012. The company won, in 2014, against the government's attempt to force the Green family and their employees to violate their deeply held religious belief that unborn babies deserve protection and that the company should have no part in funding the murder of these helpless children. President Obama's Affordable Care Act, known as Obamacare, failed to acknowledge the overriding First Amendment right to Freedom of Religion. Freedom of Religion includes religious expression everywhere—not just in church buildings as the government attempted to claim—but in the marketplace too. This victory cost David a substantial sum and nearly forced the closure of his company when government officials and judges insisted that he must be made to violate his commitment to following God's Word. Yet, David stood firm.

David has not been afraid to face societal giants: These two high-profile examples of marketplace ministry efforts and the Christian company culture they built are prominent illustrations of David's efforts to follow God's leading faithfully. From his four fundamental retailing success principles and his implementation of policies that emphasized personal accountability alongside the freedom to make decisions at low levels in the company, David grew the business. And together with his family, he wisely chose to invest those profits in promoting the Gospel message across the globe.

These initiatives continue to bear fruit to this day, in both the business and in charitable efforts. They form a remarkable testament to the God-given success of the boy who started life in "middle of nowhere."

26

Synthesizing Ministry and Business

"But seek first the kingdom of God and his righteousness,
and all these things will be added to you."
— *Matthew 6:33*

Gil Stricklin

1934-current

Throughout this book, we have explored the lives of people who have put their faith into practice in the marketplace. Our next entrepreneur got a late start in business, after retiring from a career in the government, but once he launched his business career, his faith became his business market niche. You might say this final American entrepreneur provides a unique perspective on how Christians can synthesize ministry and business to reach many future believers wandering around in the marketplace.

Gilford Stricklin—known as Gil—was born in Denison, Texas,

and worked his way through both high school and college in his hometown by working in the railroad yards. Gil received his Bachelor in Business from Baylor University in 1957 and was commissioned a second lieutenant in the United States Air Force through Baylor's ROTC. He married his wife Ann the year after graduating from college.

After his tour of duty in the Air Force, Gil returned to Texas to earn a journalism degree from Texas Christian University in 1963. Then he took a job as religion editor of the Fort Worth Star-Telegram while attending Southwestern Baptist Theological Seminary, earning both a Bachelor and Master of Divinity degrees. Even though Gil enjoyed learning, he was not a typical academic. Gil is known as having a very enthusiastic and outgoing personality.

Upon earning both divinity degrees in 1973, Gil joined the Army Chaplain Corps, serving for twenty-two years until 1994, retiring as a Colonel with thirty-seven years of combined military officer service. During his military career, he graduated from Strategic Studies Institute—the Army's highest level of education in the National Defense University—and the Command and General Staff College. In the 1970s, early in his Army career, Gil occasionally worked as a speaker for Zig Ziglar, the famous motivational speaker, over the course of seven years.

Following Gil's retirement from the Army, he worked for Dr. Billy Graham for five years traveling the world as his special assistant responsible for media relations. By this time, the Stricklins had settled in Dallas.

Over the years, even after he retired from the Army, Gil entertained multitudes of people. He attended more than 3,000 banquets and conventions as a keynote speaker across the country. He has also spoken to more than 100,000 school teachers and hundreds of business owners, as well as preaching in pulpits throughout the nation. Gil is known as a humorous speaker, a very outgoing and enthusiastic person, and someone who understands both the business world and Christian compassion. He combines motivation and a Christian message with plenty of laughter.

Transforming the Marketplace

One day in 1983, having just retired from the Convention office, Gil presented an idea to his friend Ed Bonneau: Import a model of military chaplaincy—similar to the kind he observed while holding office in the Baptist General Convention of Texas[131]—into the commercial workplace. Ed wanted to be Gil's first client. So in 1984, Gil founded Marketplace Ministries Inc. as a non-profit fee-based (rather than donation-based) charitable corporation run on Christian business principles.

The mission statement of Marketplace Ministries is as follows:

> *Marketplace Chaplains exists to share God's love in the workplace by providing an employee care service through Chaplain Teams, providing excellent chaplains,*

---

[131] During the late 1970s.

giving exceptional care to every employee.

Core Values are:

- People with exceptional care.
- Transformation with God's love.
- Marketplace with Chaplain Teams.
- Empowerment with quality training.

The approach this unusual company emphasizes is forming ongoing relationships and trust with individuals. All relationships are voluntary at the employee's choice. Companies simply pay to make the service available to all who might be interested. Company chaplains view themselves as partners with local churches, an extension of churches. They work with any denomination affirming the company's basic statement of faith—basic Christian doctrines.

How does this work in practice? Chaplains who wear easily identifiable shirts with Marketplace Ministry logos visit workplace offices, factories, and other locations of client companies to chat with employees at all levels weekly without interrupting production schedules. They often attend company-wide meetings and are integrated into the workplace. Primarily through brief friendly personal chats backed up by free literature and a phone app, the corporate chaplains meet the physical, emotional, social, and spiritual needs of employees and their families. The phone app provides both continuing training for chaplains and provides a link between chaplains and client employees in remote, on-the-road, or home-based locations. Chaplain teams are expected to serve employee family members—to be on-call and available both at work and anywhere else twenty-four hours per day, seven days per week, 365 days every year to provide care support.

While Marketplace Ministries says its chaplains observe a code of strict confidence, there are three exceptions. They are legally mandated to report certain types of information, such as when an employee threatens to harm herself/himself or other people or when an employee reveals a case of child abuse. The final exception is "when harm to the client company or its well-being is about to occur."

Business owners say the service is not typical HR and is very cost-effective, boosting morale and productivity, reducing turnover and downtime. Company owners and managers find the service builds more cooperation and trust between employees and managers, fellow workers, vendors, and customers. An increasing number of published studies indicate workers not only spend most of their waking hours in the workplace, they feel isolated from the community and traditional social connections, bringing those needs and problems into the workplace to a greater amount than previous generations did. Many companies respond by offering Employee Assistance Programs (EAPs) which consist mostly of hotlines to call or a few hours with a contracted psychologist or psychiatrist who never visits the workplace.

These same studies report 50 percent of public sector employees and only 25 percent of private-sector workers have access to EAPs, but less than seven percent actually take advantage of these services. The disconnect is due primarily to a lack of trusting personal relationships, which chaplains are ideally suited to provide. For example, a 2008 study by the Families and Work Institute found that more than 97 percent of companies with payrolls larger than 5,000 offer employee assistance programs, with anonymous counseling and referrals available by phone. Yet employees are "dramatically" more likely to use workplace chaplains than standard mental-health benefits, according to preliminary results from an ongoing study by David Miller and Faith Ngunjiri of Princeton University's Faith & Work Initiative. At least half of 1,000 employees surveyed have used the services of a workplace chaplain—far more than those who use standard assistance programs.

Gil developed a training and certification academy to assure chaplains understand how to minister in a diverse environment and understand business pressures. The academy has grown to offer fifty-five courses, ensuring chaplains are fully prepared to handle any workplace or personal situation. Chaplains provide personal confidential help to client employees and their families. They are also trained to provide post-firing counseling as well as to perform typical chaplaincy roles for funerals, hospital visits, marriages, divorce and child counseling, addictions, jail visits, and other common personal problems. Marketplace Ministries trains their chaplains to avoid employee/employer conflict advice—remaining neutral to retain the confidence and trust of both parties. Though chaplains will give managers a sense of employee concerns and corporate cultural challenges.

Marketplace Ministries provides trimester reports the first year and semi-annually after that to management with no employee names, covering both by location and company-wide the issues that employees are dealing with, in crisis or in everyday concerns. A Company Care Leader meets with the business owner to discuss key dashboard analytics and changes or trends to help the owner proactively tailor responses and resources as appropriate. Between formal reporting meetings, the owner receives critical data and stories to assist in implementing the owner's vision for care.

Reports are designed to help executives in three key areas:

· Communicate scope of employee issues impacting their lives and performance.
· Provide information on how much employees are utilizing the service and how chaplains help mitigate or solve problems.
· Provide recommendations to enhance employee care and improve corporate culture.

Chaplains are truly committed to providing Christian care ministry, not simply employee counseling. For example, one chaplain helped a single mother employee whose car was repossessed and who was about to have her house foreclosed. The chaplain refinanced and saved her house, then found people to replace her leaky roof for free, which stunned the woman. Another chaplain discussed how an increasing number of workers have no church or other support networks. Thus, they ask him to perform funerals, weddings, family counseling, and many other traditional church services.

As another chaplain explained, "Everybody has problems that

can carry over in the workplace." During times of personal crises, a surprising number of client employees seek religious comfort. Because of today's diverse work environments, chaplains do not actively evangelize, but they are always ready to share Jesus with those open to hearing the Gospel. Many chaplains assist in conducting employee Bible studies in offices and factories during lunch hours and breaks. They can also be an autonomous conduit for financial assistance to employees and their families from Christian business owners.

Chaplains have found a tremendous openness in all the workplaces where they contract to work, even among atheists and employees with non-Christian beliefs. Employees are often stunned that the company would show such deeply personal care. Nearly all clients are Christian entrepreneurs who truly want to implement biblical principles to care for employees, vendors, customers, and others they work with.

A Marketplace Ministry executive stated, "Our primary mission is to care for people. We want to show Christian love and compassion for those employees." Chaplains will meet at hospitals, homes, jails, nursing homes, and anywhere an employee needs help or just a sympathetic ear. They have a network of resources to tap into. If an employee in one part of the nation has a parent who has a sudden medical emergency, another corporate chaplain can be at the parent's side within an hour. If an employee seeks a different faith for more information, chaplains can refer them to an outside source. The vast majority of corporate chaplains and the entrepreneurs who hire or contract them are Christians, nearly all Protestants.

As Founder, Gil has served as President and CEO of Marketplace Ministries. Today he is Chairman and has turned over daily management responsibilities to a president he brought into the company in 2015. The company has grown rapidly: Gil had created a subsidiary to serve an industry he understands well. In 2010 he founded Railroad Chaplains of America Inc.

With its national headquarters based in Dallas, the company has expanded nationwide. Marketplace Ministries employs over 2,700 chaplains, up 50 percent since 2005, located in all fifty states as well as international operations. The company services more than 750,000 employees plus their families among nearly 900 client companies ranging from three employees to firms with nearly 30,000 in more than 3,500 locations. Thus far, the company has provided over 5,000,000 hours of counseling.

Gil's vision is to treat client employees holistically based upon Matthew 6:33, "But seek first the kingdom of God and his righteousness, and all these things will be added to you." In other words, by caring personally for each workplace individual, not only does each get to experience examples of Christian caring, some opportunities will arise to share the Gospel. Company executives routinely share with their chaplain staff how many client employees and their family members come to faith in Christ through chaplain care and witnessing efforts.

Not all corporate chaplaincy services are outsourcing contracts with independent chaplaincy companies. For example, Tyson Foods is a publicly-traded company with its own in-house chaplaincy program started in 2000, employing 115 chaplains, the largest known corporate chaplaincy program. But most chaplains work for privately held companies, some of which are billion-dollar enterprises, so Tyson might not be the biggest employer of company chaplains. Yet, the corporate chaplaincy firms are a cost-effective approach for many companies, particularly smaller firms, to carry out their owners' visions for marketplace ministry, thanks to the original vision and efforts of Gil Stricklin.

One of their closest competitors, Corporate Chaplains of America (CCA), based in Wake Forest, North Carolina, has a similar mission: "build caring relationships with the hope of gaining permission to share the life-changing Good News of Jesus Christ in a non-threatening manner." That company, founded by Mark Cress, who has both an MBA with extensive corporate and entrepreneurial experience plus a master's in divinity degree, is also structured as a non-profit corporation. CCA has a twenty-one-acre ministry campus. The company has over 150 active full-time chaplains and even more part-time chaplains, serving thousands of employees across forty states and internationally. CCA also has its own training facility to assure high quality and marketplace understanding.

These multi-million dollar large ministry organizations are not the only participants in this fast-growing service sector. An increasing number of smaller entrants start up on a regular basis. For example, Capital Chaplains, which began in 2005, not only provides corporate chaplaincy services to companies in the Wisconsin area it also produces a guide on how evangelists and ministers can start a corporate chaplaincy company.

269

Likewise, The Corporate Chaplain is another such smaller firm, as is Chaplains Associates Inc. Corporate Chaplaincy Consulting is yet another company that provides both corporate chaplaincy services and personal training for pastors wanting to enter this field. Some of these companies are structured as for-profit businesses, while others are non-profit corporations.[132]

Demand continues to explode as more companies seek holistic help for their employees, expanding well beyond the United States. The workplace chaplain movement exists in the UK, Germany, Switzerland, Australia, Canada, Hong Kong, and several other nations—bringing comfort, care, support, and hope to a hurting world.

---

[132] The difference really amounts to just a tax break versus greater operational flexibility and perhaps a personal preference by the company owner since the counseling and support services are the same in either structural model.

27

To the Ends of the Earth

"But you will receive power when the Holy Spirit has come upon you,
and you will be my witnesses...to the end of the earth."
— *Acts 1:8*

Most of the world's entrepreneurs, including most Christian entrepreneurs, have come from the United States due to the economic, environmental, and social factors encouraging entrepreneurs, as discussed at the beginning of this book. Yet Christian entrepreneurs can be found on every inhabited continent.[133] This chapter provides a few examples of how Christian entrepreneurs worldwide are transforming their nations and continents, although personal information on such accomplishments is much harder to find outside America. To give you a glimpse into Christian entrepreneurship world-wide, we will uncover brief biographies of Christian business heroes working on three different continents—Asia, Europe,

---

[133] Occasionally, one visits the uninhabited continent.

and Africa.

Cher Wang: 1958-current

Cher Wang is a native of Taipei, Taiwan. She chose to study abroad, earning a Bachelor of Economics from the University of California at Berkeley in 1981. She returned to Taipei to work for First International Computer in 1982.

Unlike most entrepreneurs profiled in this book, Cher did not start life in poverty. Cher's dad, Wang Yung-ching, launched Formosa Plastics Corp, a plastics and petrochemicals conglomerate. When he died in 2008, Cher became one of the wealthiest people in Taiwan. While Cher did not start in poverty, she chose to actively build both her business career and her philanthropic career, rather than rest upon inherited wealth.

In 1987, she became a co-founder of VIA Technologies Corporation, a major global manufacturer of integrated chipsets. In 1997 she started another company, HTC Corporation, with a partner. HTC has grown rapidly and now manufactures almost 17 percent of all smartphones sold in the United States, in addition to capturing an expanding segment of the electronic circuitry market in many other nations.

Cher took personal control over VIA when its executives lost a court case over the manufacturing of an anti-hack chip, which allowed the mainland communist Chinese government to conduct surveillance on human rights activists in 2014.

She halted this facilitation with human rights violations and provided daily leadership for HTC rather than settling for a continued board chair position of oversight.

Cher has contributed over $200 million USD to her Charity Foundations over the years. In 2011 she donated $28.1 million USD to help launch Guizhou Forerunner College in southwest China via her VIA company's Faith-Hope-Love Foundation. This non-profit college provides three years of free or very low-cost education to students from low-income families. She has indicated an interest in starting similar college models throughout China.

Cher has also made significant donations to her alma mater, UC-Berkeley, to support condensed matter physics. She has provided the funding to found a collaborative program between the psychology departments of UC-Berkeley and Tsinghua University in Beijing. Other education-related charitable gifts include donating 6,000 HTC Flyer tablet personal computers to sixty Taipei high schools in 2012.

Along with her husband, Wen-Chi Chen, Cher continues to be an active and enthusiastic philanthropist, although she prefers to avoid the spotlight. In 2014, Forbes magazine estimated her wealth at $8.8 billion USD as the wealthiest person in Taiwan and the 54th most powerful woman in the world. For all that success, she and her husband are well known as Christian philanthropists in the predominantly Buddhist and Taoist island nation of Taiwan. They are active in sharing their faith through charity efforts in communist China.

Dr. Imre Somody: 1954-current

Across the world from Cher, Dr. Imre Somody provides another example of Christian entrepreneurship. When the communist government in Hungary collapsed in 1989, Imre—a
trained chemist from the pharmaceutical drug manufacturer
Chinoin—built upon a Swiss research project to develop an
effervescent vitamin tablet. Shortly after that, he founded
Pharmavit to promote his Plussez brand of vitamin drinks,
vitamin tablets, and other health products.

The company grew rapidly in the turbulent days of the country's re-introduction to free markets. Plussez quickly captured
51 percent of Hungary's vitamin market, with one out of every
four citizens using his products daily. In 1995, the company
doubled sales throughout Eastern Europe to $10 million USD.
Only two years later, he had doubled that sales figure again, in
addition to another $10 million USD from the domestic market.

Through clever Olympic medal winner endorsements, Imre
captured over 35 percent of the vitamin market in Poland and
Romania, expanding into Russia, Ukraine, Vietnam, and a
growing number of other companies. He negotiated a joint
agreement with American company Bristol-Meyers Squibb
which purchased a 9.9 percent stake in Pharmavit in late 1995.
Bristol-Meyers has since been assisting Pharmavit to build
a worldwide distribution and marketing system throughout
Asia and South America.

In 1996 Imre sold Pharmavit, earning so many tens of millions
of dollars in the private sale that he began to consider a second

career trying to transform Hungary into a successful European country similar to those in the prosperous western portion of the continent. As an atheist, he had two motivations: First, he wanted to gain the respect of most fellow Hungarians by showing them he was not solely all about making money. Second, he desired to gain a new sense of purpose for his life. Thus he embarked upon a new career as a generous philanthropist, working primarily through donations to many different Hungarian charities.

Later, Imre realized some of those charities in the chaotic post-communist and still-transitioning Hungarian society were less than transparent and trustworthy. He lost most of his wealth and almost had to sell his house to support his family. He had lost confidence in his abilities and became fearful that he could not succeed again. However, in 2014 Imre attended a retreat where he encountered Jesus and received the freedom from worry and fear that faith in Christ can provide. Imre wondered what his wife would think about this sudden conversion. He was overjoyed to find that she too had become a Christian that same weekend!

As a new Christian, Imre cut back all his business efforts and focused on launching a new coffee shop called Cafe Central in Budapest. This coffee shop is not what Americans or most Westerners might think of as a coffee shop. It is several stories tall and has a live theater inside the large building, as many such cafes in Hungary have. Since it is a privately held company, Imre has not published its financial status. However, the company appears to be a multi-million dollar enterprise, which allows him to present a prominent Christian example in Budapest.

Imre is learning to provide a biblical example of business. This can be very difficult when dealing with employees who grew up with the socialist entitlement mentality. They expect him to give them money for not working: They think Christians are supposed to act that way.

How can a Christian entrepreneur in such a situation share the biblical message of dignity and a sense of accomplishment through work while conveying an accurate idea of true charity help?

Imre is one of a growing number of Christian convert entrepreneurs in such transition societies providing living examples of Christ-like caring and training for those who have no guidance in their lives and who might become open to a radical life-changing healthy transformation as Imre found.

Strive Masiyiwa: 1961-current

From the European continent where Christianity is struggling, we turn to the vibrant continent of Africa. In the 21st century, Africa has become the continent where Christianity is growing the fastest. Strive Masiyiwa displays a clear example of why.

This Zimbabwean entrepreneur attended primary school in Zambia, then completed his secondary schooling in Scotland, following which he earned a degree in Electrical Engineering from the University of Wales. After seventeen years living abroad, Strive returned to his native Zimbabwe in 1984.[134] Upon returning home, Strive worked briefly as a telecoms engineer for the government telephone company.

Shortly after that, Strive launched his first corporation with just $75 USD. In less than five years, his startup had become one of the nation's largest electrical engineering businesses. The mobile phone industry was just beginning in America. He was eager to bring that new technology to Africa, envisioning the vast savings possible from avoiding the cost of building an expensive legacy landline network like those in Western countries. He saw that Africa could skip over that high-cost step to jump directly to lower-cost wireless communications. However, the Prime Minister/dictator, Robert Mugabe, would not grant a telephony license to compete with the government. Strive fought a five-year legal battle for freedom of expression to win the license from the Constitutional Court of Zimbabwe, which had not yet fallen under the control of the dictator. The legal fight nearly bankrupted him.

Finally, 14 years after beginning his quest to bring affordable communication to his country and his continent, Strive was able to start his wireless phone company, albeit with heavily depleted finances. For a second time, he was starting with nearly nothing. In 1998, Strive connected his first wireless customer to his new network showing the fruits of his hard-won legal battle.

---

[134] This was four years after the troubled country achieved independence from the white minority that wrested control from Britain in 1965 and suppressed the rights and economic opportunities of the black majority under the national name of Rhodesia.

To reward network subscribers—well beyond substantially cutting communications costs below what the government charged—Strive also listed the company, Econet Wireless, on the local stock exchange, letting customers share in the rapidly growing profits. Within a few years, Econet became the second largest company in Zimbabwe by market capitalization. It still dominates the economy.

The company had some financial setbacks for a couple of years after that, and Strive was forced, reluctantly, to lay off about one hundred workers. To put this in context, from the first year of independence in 1980 the Prime Minister/dictator, Mugabe, mismanaged the economy. By 2003, the economy was contracting by 18 percent annually, and inflation rose from 32 percent in 1998 to over 11,200,000 percent in 2008 when the government stopped reporting its failures.

Unemployment reached over 80 percent by 2007. In January 2013, the Finance Ministry reported the national treasury balance was down to just $217 USD. The government could not even afford to print the $100 million ZWL[135] banknotes that people used to buy ordinary goods for survival. On top of all this, Mugabe committed tremendous widespread human rights abuses until he was removed by a military coup in 2017.

Under these horrendous circumstances, it is truly amazing and a testament to Strive's determination and Christian principles that he led his company to success and laid off only one hundred out of thousands of employees during this period

---

[135] The Zimbabwean dollar.

of crushing economic and civil rights catastrophe. During this period Mugabe also spent the equivalent of hundreds of millions of US dollars participating in the Democratic Republic of the Congo (DRC) civil war. This later led Strive to bring mobile phone service and jobs to the DRC to relieve the suffering of many people in that troubled and impoverished nation.

In 1993, Strive formed Econet Wireless Group as a South African corporation. This was one year before the apartheid era of white minority bigotry against the black majority ended. Again, this seems like a brave move. Perhaps Strive was thinking about bringing greater opportunities to people in a nation on the cusp of significant change. Maybe he was trying to keep his international expansion efforts out of reach of the Zimbabwe dictator's ability to expropriate them. Whatever his reasoning might have been at that time, Strive established his headquarters in Johannesburg, South Africa as a diversified telecommunications group. His rapid success allowed him to expand operations throughout Africa, Europe, South America, and the East Asia Pacific Rim. Services also expanded to include mobile and fixed telephone services, broadband internet, satellite communications, optical fiber networks, and mobile payment systems. New subsidiaries multiplied like rabbits.

When Strive received his first telephony license from the Zimbabwe government in 1998, more than 70 percent of all residents had never even heard a ringtone in their entire lives. This was true in many other African countries to which he expanded operations, bringing newfound freedom and knowledge at very affordable prices. He launched EcoCash in 2005 to provide a phone-based payment and funds transfer service to the NGOs.[136] They were trying to bring cash and payment for necessities to the people in war-torn Burundi.

After the Burundi war, the service proved so popular and cost-effective that by 2011 Strive opened it to any individual or company who wanted to use it. Again, he lowered costs for the people of Africa and skipped an expensive stage of banking development. Most Africans did not have (and in many nations, many still do not have) bank accounts. This phone-based payment system provided a cheap, fast bank-equivalent that offered better banking services than many African banks. Nobody had such a service at that time anywhere in Africa, and no entrepreneur except Strive envisioned such a vast advancement.

He returned to his first hard-fought achievement. Within 18 months of Econet signing its initial customer, over 31 percent of all Zimbabwean adults were registered with Strive's company. By late 2017 he had 6.7 million registered customers in Zimbabwe using his service regularly, capturing 80 percent of the domestic market, or 52 percent of all citizens, including youth. In 2013 Strive purchased TN Bank Zimbabwe, a small local bank, renaming it Steward Bank, growing the bank enormously to support his international phone-based innovative payments system. The next year he purchased Telecel in Burundi and another Telecel company in the Central African Republic for $65 million USD. To keep flexibility for

---

[136] Non-Governmental Organizations, a United Nations term for private charities.

operating all his companies according to biblical principles, Strive has not listed any of these several dozen corporations on any stock exchanges except the original Zimbabwe company.

In 2000, Strive moved from Johannesburg, South Africa, to London, England, but he still maintains his international head-quarters in Johannesburg. The companies now operate in over twenty countries, including the United States. Strive's huge job creation wave, innovative delivery service, and economic improvements in the face of tremendous government threats, economic disasters, wars, and human rights abuses—among the many nations in which he operates—is a testament to what a Christian entrepreneur can accomplish in lifting and transforming multiple societies while staying focused on Jesus. This is especially true since Strive has turned down deals worth hundreds of millions of US dollars rather than participate in the corruption so common in many African governments.

As a result of all these impressive achievements, Forbes magazine estimated Strive's net worth, several years ago, at approximately $1.7 billion USD. Yet all this economic improvement and business achievement is less than half of the story. Strive is widely known as one of the most generous African philanthropists. He was quoted in a July 30, 2009 article in the London-based newspaper The Guardian explaining his Christian faith in the marketplace:

> Christianity is a value system that calls on me to be compassionate, it calls on me to help the weak. I generate a lot of money for me and my shareholders

and people who have been associated with me, but that cannot be an end in itself.

He provides scholarships to over 100,000 young Africans through his family foundation. He supports more than 40,000 orphans with educational initiatives, plus sponsoring African students to attend American, United Kingdom, and Chinese universities. In recent years he has concentrated on personally mentoring young African entrepreneurs. The 2.5 million Facebook followers of his business advice page make him the most engaged and followed of any business leader in the world. He also funds public health and agriculture initiatives throughout the African continent.

Strive serves on the boards of The Rockefeller Foundation, US Council on Foreign Relations International Advisory Board, Asia Society, Alliance for a Green Revolution in Africa, Micronutrient Initiative of Canada, EBOLA Fund, Morehouse College, Pan African Strategic Institute, United States Holocaust Memorial Museum's Committee on Conscience, and two United Nations advisory panels. In response to a major Ebola outbreak in 2014, he became the first business leader to organize and set up the first Pan-African fundraising campaign—resulting in the largest known contingency of African healthcare workers to combat the spread of the pandemic. This dwarfed the Ebola humanitarian attempts of all governments and international governmental organizations that had attempted relief up to that point.

Strive is one of the most generous African philanthropists.

He built one of the largest support programs for educating orphans in Africa. He also participates in the joint initiative Giving Pledge, founded and initially funded by Bill and Melinda Gates with Warren Buffett. Strive also donates to multiple campaigns against HIV/AIDS,[137] cervical cancer, malnutrition, and Ebola. He also supports the environmental cleanup and is a joint founder along with Sir Richard Branson of the environmental group Carbon War Room. He is also chairman of AGRA, which supports Africa's small farmers. As co-chair of Grow Africa, he has helped attract $15 billion USD of investments into African agriculture.

There is even more charitable giving of money and time. Africa Progress Panel, a UK and UN-sponsored independent Swiss non-profit agency, asked him to join as one of the only ten members. This agency advises and advocates to top-level African and UN leaders for equitable and sustainable development throughout Africa. It also promotes rule of law policies to enforce sustainability and stability. Strive's particular role is facilitating coalition building and knowledge sharing to influence policies for lasting improvements.

Strive has received many international awards and praise for his business expertise and Christian philanthropy and is considered one of Africa's most generous humanitarians. 2014 Fortune magazine named him one of the top fifty most influential business leaders globally. The International Rescue Committee awarded him the Freedom Award in 2015 for extraordinary contributions towards refugee support and

---

[137] An epidemic in much of Africa.

consistent advocacy in the causes of liberty, individual free-dom, and dignity. Fortune magazine in 2017 named him the 33rd most effective of the world's greatest leaders in all fields. Regardless of all these awards and recognitions for his workplace and societal efforts to help millions of people and improve their quality of life.

The Most Important Recognition

However, the most important recognition for this—or any of the other Christian entrepreneurs we've read about in these pages or those who strive to live out their faith around the world—is to hear upon arrival in heaven Jesus speaking the words of Matthew 25:23.

> ...Well done, good and faithful servant. You have been faithful over a little; I will set you over much. Enter into the joy of your master.

May each one of us live lives that are worthy of these words.

28

You!

*"But be doers of the word, and not hearers only,
deceiving yourselves....
[the one who] acts, he will be blessed in his doing."*
— James 1:22-25

The Next Entrepreneur

Throughout this book, we explored the benefits of entrepreneurship, its history, and its Christian philosophical basis. Put together, we studied how this creates the perfect incubator for amazing advancements in society. Hopefully, you were thrilled and intrigued by the examples of these couple dozen Christian entrepreneur practitioners. There are many thousands more from all industries, nations, various time periods, economic conditions, and nearly every other possible starting point one can imagine.

Many of the companies that created the products and services we take for granted today came from Christian entrepreneurs—more than we could include in this book: Tom Monaghan of Domino's Pizza, Bo Pilgrim of Pilgrim's Pride chicken, Henry Parsons Crowell of Quaker Oats cereal, Marion Wade of Service Master, Sir. John Templeton of Templeton Mutual Funds, David Steward of World Wide Technologies, Norm Miller of Interstate Batteries, and countless others.

At some point, we must pause the entrepreneurial stories and take action on what we have learned. As the Bible points out—particularly in the book of James—faith without action is worthless. Faith loves to give back what it has itself received. Perhaps God might be calling you to join the illustrious and exciting ranks of Christian entrepreneurs. What might such a calling look like?

There is no unique set of characteristics or experiences to improve your likelihood of success. Entrepreneurs have found success in a wide variety of opportunities. There seem to be a few shared preparatory experiences—growing up in poverty, facing adversity and "failing"—as the world incorrectly defines that word—one or more times, and for many switching industries. But even those experiences are not universal.

Yet, taken as a whole, Christian entrepreneurs seem to be committed to sharing the material and spiritual gifts God provides when they first become Christians—frequently long before they achieve monetary success. Most are determined to invest that wealth in permanent heavenly wealth rather than fleeting earthly ones. And they give not only of their monetary wealth but also of the wealth of their talents and time.

Did you notice another theme among these Christian entrepreneurs? They seek efficiency and effectiveness. This also applies to charitable giving. Whether leading a for-profit business or a charitable corporation, each Christian entrepreneur is keenly aware of their stewardship responsibilities to God. Most had not read about the formal leadership theory of Quadruple Bottom Line Goals—financial, social, environmental, and spiritual. Still, they all pursued such an approach in their business, charitable, and personal spheres of influence. At the same time, they were calculated risk-takers. While attempting outstanding achievements, they approached those lofty goals in faith, trusting in God to see them through.

In other words, these Christian entrepreneurs saw no artificial separation of business and faith. They refused to settle for a mediocre one or two-dimensional life. Instead, each pursued the richness of a full multi-dimensional life, pursuing societal and spiritual benefits for as many people as they could reach. God rewarded them with great monetary success, yet they all were focused not on money but on how they could help others, both temporally and eternally.

What makes a successful Christian entrepreneur? It depends. What is the definition of success? For the Christian entrepreneur, it is not any material thing. Yet, they provide material goods, services, and benefits to themselves and their employees. It's an astounding paradox.

How to resolve it? The Christian recognizes that en-

287

trepreneurial success requires a moral, biblically-based free enterprise environment because entrepreneurial success is an expression of *imago dei*—the image of God impressed in us by our Creator, including creativity and a desire to know God. Christian entrepreneurs are innovators, calculated risk-takers, and people who deeply care about others to a generous and often sacrificial extent.

My hope in writing this book is that it will inspire future entrepreneurs to take action. Some, of course, will see these exhilarating biographies as merely interesting business history or philosophy. But it is my hope that some readers will learn from these examples—imitating their successes and learning from their failures. These examples of faith put into action can be an inspiration to achieve your own God-given calling for ministry in the marketplace, where harvest opportunities are perhaps greater than those reaped by churches.

Getting Started

Not sure how to get started? There are many books on starting a business. You might find helpful my companion book to this one—*Transforming Entrepreneurship: How to build a world-changing business as a Christian.*[138]

Here are some possible next steps:

---

[138] Also available at Entrepreneur Institute.

- Seek out a Christian business owner to mentor you
- Develop leadership and sales skills
- Create a sustainable, innovative idea
- Contact one of the Christian business organizations listed below
- Consider taking the program of online courses provided by my Entrepreneur College designed specifically to help Christians who want to become entrepreneurs—or business owners who want to incorporate a Christian marketplace witness into their existing businesses.

There are a growing number of business organizations for Christian entrepreneurs. The two oldest and largest are:

- Fellowship of Companies for Christ International - www.fcci.org
- C12 Group – www.c12group.com

If you conduct business globally there is an organization that includes many Christian entrepreneurs, although it is not exclusively for entrepreneurs: International Christian Chamber of Commerce - www.iccc.net

All of these associations, domestic and international, have materials and local Bible study groups as well as regional, national, and international conferences addressing Biblical perspectives and situations entrepreneurs face daily.

Unfortunately, *none of these groups are focused on mentoring newer entrepreneurs to launch and grow new enterprises that also share Christian love in the marketplace.* That is why I have founded a charitable global research institute to help new entrepreneurs:

Entrepreneur Leadership Institute.

If you would like further information on resources for starting or growing your entrepreneurial organization, visit our website at:

www.EntrepreneurLeadership.net

Please also feel free to email me personally at:

books@EntrepreneurLeadership.net

I'm looking forward to hearing from you!

Entrepreneur Leadership Institute is transforming entrepreneurship by sponsoring research on entrepreneurial leadership with an emphasis on a Christian perspective and sharing this information with aspiring and current entrepreneurs—like you—around the world.

In addition to books produced by Entrepreneur Leadership Institute we are also developing a growing number of resources for entrepreneurs from a Christian perspective, such as:

- Blog – brief insights on specific topics.
- Podcasts – short talks on broad business and marketplace ministry areas.

- Webinars – longer workshops which are deep dive immersions into particular aspects of starting and leading a marketplace ministry business or nonprofit organization.

Entrepreneur Leadership Institute is here to provide the training and support to set you on the path to creating the kind of business that can transform society and spread the Gospel.

Just as the entrepreneurs in this book each had a unique vision, set of obstacles to overcome, and a calling from God, so do you. Is he calling you to take action? If you are saved, God is at work transforming your life. He has called you to participate in that work and in the work of transforming the world.

The question I'll leave you with is this: Is God calling you today to transforming entrepreneurship?

About the Author

Dr. Kenneth R. Lenz has started many companies, non-profit organizations and is a co-founder of a municipal government. He is also a CPA who has started, led, and sold several accounting and consulting firms across the United States. His firms have focused on providing services to smaller and rapidly growing entrepreneurial firms in various parts of the United States and several other continents. In addition, he earned a Ph.D. in entrepreneurial leadership.

From this unique background, he has studied and been deeply involved with entrepreneurship from the perspective of a serial entrepreneur in a variety of industries, as an adviser to many small business owners, and as a government official writing laws that affected business owners, in the profit-oriented as well as social entrepreneurship (social and governmental) sectors of the economy.

Dr. Lenz has also taught online business, entrepreneurship, and leadership courses on the bachelors, masters, and doctoral levels for universities in America and Europe. From these many-faceted viewpoints on entrepreneurship, he has also been involved in the international marketplace ministry movement for more than 20 years as a Christian entrepreneur.

Currently, he is chairman and founder of the Entrepreneur Leadership Institute. This small international research institute conducts innovative research in entrepreneurial leadership and shares those findings with entrepreneurs worldwide to help them improve society, both temporally and eternally. He is also developing a division of the Entrepreneur Leadership Institute which will offer training for individuals desiring to start and grow new businesses that can also engage in sharing the Gospel in the marketplace.